To one of my favorite bear
hunting partners

you might recognize
the world famous outdoorsman in the photos on
pages 73 & 88. Just remember
who made you famous.

afore ole buddy,
Jerry Meyer

BEAR HUNTING

BEAR HUNTING

Jerry Meyer

Stackpole Books

BEAR HUNTING

Copyright © 1983 by Jerry Meyer

Published by
STACKPOLE BOOKS
Cameron and Kelker Streets
P. O. Box 1831
Harrisburg, PA 17105

Printed in the U.S.A.

Library of Congress Cataloging in Publication Data

Meyer, Jerry, 1939–
    Bear hunting.

    Includes index.
    1. Bear hunting.   I. Title.
SK295.M49 1983   799.2'774446   83–12533
ISBN 0-8117-0218-9

To Dick and Mother T., my world record class in-laws.

Contents

Foreword

Few outdoor experiences compare with a sportsman's first bear hunt. Bears represent North America's most dangerous and cunning quarry, and a successful ending to such an adventure leaves a feeling of accomplishment unrivaled in the outdoor world.

Jerry Meyer's request that I write the introduction to his book came, ironically, only a few days after I had killed the last bear of my hunting career. When the smoke from my muzzleloader cleared that day, I had finally taken the monster black bear that had eluded me for twenty years, and that ended it for me.

I am not against bear hunting. I love it, and I believe that every hunter owes it to himself to experience the ultimate in North American hunting adventure. It's just that I know I am never going to get a bigger trophy, and I prefer to have other hunters share the enjoyment bears have brought to me. I will guide bear hunters until I can no longer take to the woods, but I myself will not kill another bear.

If any single outside source would have helped my twenty-year quest for a trophy bear, I think it would be this book. *Bear Hunting* is a no-nonsense approach to the sport. There are no hero stories—just a common sense, how-to-do-it treatise on stalking and taking a bruin. It leans heavily toward the black bear, and rightfully so. Perhaps ninety-five percent of bear hunters pursue the black bear, and those that seek the Kodiak, the grizzly and the polar bear will most certainly have the benefit of outfitters and guides.

This book has been written for the beginning bear hunter, whether he be an archer or a rifleman. Among the many areas it covers are hunting with hounds, baiting, and using tree stands and blinds. Unlike cloven-hoofed animals, bear are difficult to track, and the author carefully covers the fine points of sign reading which are critical to a successful hunt. Perhaps most important, he covers the diet of bears. If there is any weakness in a bear's natural defenses, it is in his ravenous appetite. Bears will eat almost anything, but they have distinct preferences and the knowledge of those preferences gives the hunter an edge under certain conditions.

Bear hunting gets in the blood. It is sometimes frustrating and always challenging. The information in Meyer's book will, most certainly, give the hunter an additional advantage that can well be the difference between success and failure.

                John Long
                Host, "Outdoor World" television series

Acknowledgments

Many people contributed time and effort in writing this book. I know that I will neglect a few.

I would like to express special thanks to: John Long, my favorite bear hunting partner and the man who has taught me so much about the bears of the far north; Dr. Mike Pelton of the University of Tennessee, who supplied so much useful information and also made it possible for me to work in the field with biologists doing bear research; Joel Arrington; Blue Boar Lodge; and the state of North Carolina. The staffs of Great Smoky Mountains, Glacier, Yellowstone, and several other national parks were very helpful in providing information and assisting with logistics.

Some other folks and outfits who were helpful were Canada North Outfitters, Dave Carlock, Roy Wilson, Kathy Fish, Oak Duke, Brian Spencer, Don Pfitzer, Bear Archery Company, Remington Arms, Winchester Arms, Federal Cartridge Corporation, Skunks Unlimited, Baker

xii   *Acknowledgment*

Manufacturing Company, Gary Ginther, Gary Bohochek, Dr. Jerry Weaver, Dr. Oris Brannan, and Dave Elliott.

Last but not least, I would like to thank two very special ladies: my wife, Katherine, who tolerated book manuscript scattered all over the house for the better part of twelve months; and Judith Schnell, my editor, who took a stack of misspelled manuscript and made it into a book. (I also want to thank Judith for her patience while the manuscript was on my desk and should have already been on hers.)

Introduction

When the folks at Stackpole asked me to write a book on bear hunting, my first reaction was, "How could I ever get a firm grip on such a broad subject, which covers hunting all species of bear from the Arctic Ocean to the Gulf of Mexico?" After much deliberation, I decided to try and provide just the essential information that would allow the reader to become a bear hunter himself.

I wanted to write a book that would deal with the practical aspects of bear hunting, avoiding as much as possible sensationalism and man-eating bear horror stories, while still making readers aware of the destructive capabilities that bears possess. I have tried to limit "hero stories" about my own accomplishments, and focus instead on errors that would contribute to your education.

To the best of my limited ability, I have tried to accomplish these objectives. I hope this volume will start you on a long career of hunting the most exciting game animal in North America.

1

Bear Hunting: The Adrenaline-Pumping, Heart-Thumping Experience

If you read this book and decide you want to try bear hunting, then I fear you are doomed to a lifetime of addiction to the habit. Once you have seen your first bear up close outside of a cage, all other outdoor endeavors will pale in comparison.

I have not hunted all the big game in North America, but I have pursued a good portion of it, including deer, wild turkey, and elk, and I have had no other species of fish, fowl, or antlered game generate the thrill of going bear hunting. I consider the bear to be one of the most challenging game animals to hunt in the entire world.

Bears have the best nose in the woods, good hearing, and better eyesight than most hunters believe. Bears are more evasive, even shy, in their normal habits than other big game animals. When was the last time you strolled right up on a bear in the thick cover they hang out in? (I am not referring here to the roadside panhandler bears or park bears, but wild bears.) The potential for injury to the hunter adds

A bear camp in the Colorado high country is the stuff that bear hunter's dreams are made of. Your chances of making this dream come true are very good if you learn the whens, wheres, and hows of bear hunting.

additional spice not just to the hunt, but to every minute you spend in bear country.

The bear has been touted as a clown, like Br'er Bear, Winnie-the-Pooh, and Yogi Bear. Movies and TV shows such as *Gentle Ben* and *Grizzly Adams* have endowed bears with human characteristics and depicted them as friends and companions. This type of exposure has helped propagate the general belief that bears are buffoons and not a danger to humans. However, many people consider each and every bear to be a vicious man eater that will drag any human he can catch off into the bush, where the victim will slowly be chewed to death.

Bears have qualified for both these categories. But membership in either of these extreme variations in behavior is rare. Most bears would fall somewhere in between the two extremes, with the vast majority being shy, retiring creatures who would avoid detection or confrontation with man at any cost. Many unpleasant social encounters result from both man and bear coming in contact, with neither being aware of the other's presence until they suddenly bump into each other. There is a good chance that the bear will flee, but in which direction is open for debate.

There are very few absolutes when it comes to predicting what any individual animal will do under any given set of circumstances. This is especially true of bears. The aggressive behavior of rogue bears can usually be explained by an abscessed tooth, a painful wound (often inflicted by other bears), loss of natural food source, or a sow protecting her cubs. Sometimes a bear attack is classified as unprovoked. But who can say that the mere appearance of a salmon fisherman on a brown bear's fishing turf is not provocation?

Bears, more than any other form of wildlife I know of, defy generalized statements about behavior. The only thing that is consistently predictable about bears is their unpredictability. Whenever you tell yourself that you have bears figured out and you will know how they will behave—that is when you will get into big trouble! Bears are individuals, and you must always be prepared for them to do the unexpected.

Grizzlies and brown bears have a reputation for being mankillers. I would rank the grizzly right behind the leopard as being the animal I would least like to press a charge. But in spite of reputation, more people have been killed by that clown of the forest, the lowly black bear, than by grizzlies or browns. Generally, this is mostly due to the fact that there are more black bears than browns or grizzlies and that blacks are more accessible to people. On a one-to-one, individual basis, browns and grizzlies are certainly more dangerous to man than blacks, but that potential for a fatal attack by a black bear still exists. The hunter who takes that potential lightly could easily end up a mortality statistic.

Food is the single factor that leads to black bears killing people. Tame blacks that feed at dumps or raid campgrounds soon lose their natural fear of men. This is understandable since an unarmed man is no match for even a smallish bear with mayhem in his heart.

On the opposite end of the spectrum is the truly wild bear that has never seen a human and views this tall, ungainly creature as just another form of groceries. Most unprovoked fatal attacks by wild bears usually result in the victim being partially eaten. Often those victims which are not eaten will be cached, or stored, for later consumption. A bear does this by raking leaves and debris over his kill to protect it until he can return and dine at his leisure. Caching is most often done by grizzlies.

Legends about bears eating people abound wherever bears and people share the same territory. This cabin in northern Ontario belonged to an elderly man known as the "Old Russian." A friend came by once to find the cabin deserted, with evidence on the front door of forced entry by a bear. The body was never found.

I know of no other big game animal that can be legally hunted by so many different methods—with hounds, over a bait, with bow and arrow, handgun, shotgun, pistol, or stalking. You can hunt polar bears on an ice floe by dog sled, or you can chase a black bear in central Florida behind a pack of baying hounds while you are in shirt sleeves. You can hunt black bears in the Alaska panhandle or sixty miles from New York City. Bear hunters even get two seasons in many states and provinces. Unlike hunters of antlered game, who must wait from fall to fall, we bear hunters have both a fall and a spring hunting season.

There are probably not as many brown bears that will square ten feet, or grizzlies that will square nine, or blacks that will square seven, but population-wise, total numbers are probably higher than they have been since the early part of this century.

Black bears are now protected in many states and provinces that paid bounties on them just over a decade ago. It wasn't too long ago that professional hunters were hired in the Northwest to reduce the black bear population. Many southeastern states have opened a bear season in the last decade that had been closed since the early part of this century.

Another advantage of bear hunting is that it can be tailored to fit any budget. Most hunters are within driving distance of territory that has black bear hunting. The nonresident license for bear hunting is a small fraction of what antlered game tags cost. In Ontario, for example, you can get a nonresident alien black bear license for twenty-five bucks; a moose license will cost you $200.

If a man can scrape up the cash, he can have a $7,000 grizzly hunt in Alaska or the Canadian Rockies that will no doubt be the highlight of his hunting career. For somewhere between $3,500 and $7,000 he can hunt the giant brown bears of Alaska from the relative comfort of a boat cruising the shoreline. For "Mr. Big Bucks" there is the high adventure of going out on the ice of the Arctic Ocean in pursuit of the great white polar bear. This not only requires a major financial investment but also a substantial contribution in stamina and resolve.

The high tab on many of the Alaskan and Canadian wilderness hunts is due to several factors. In many areas, registered guides have a quota of, say, six grizzlies a year which may be harvested by their clients. Therefore, an outfitter may only guide six paying clients a year. These six clients must absorb the cost of maintaining a string of pack horses, camp outfitting and related salaries for packers and wranglers,

Dr. Jerry Weaver, shown here approaching a downed bear, proclaimed his first bear kill to be his most exciting outdoor experience. No doubt it can be yours also.

plus a profit for the outfitter. The number of people who can kill grizzlies and browns is limited by the various quotas set in the respective management areas; thus the old "supply and demand" concept comes into play. The demand for a trophy class grizzly or brown bear greatly exceeds the supply; consequently the price of the game goes up to what the market will bear.

Since the price of a trip is so very high, a hunter should not be bashful about requesting extensive references from a prospective outfitter. You should also get in writing, a contract if you will, exactly and specifically what services the guide is providing. You wouldn't buy a $7,000 pig in a poke, so don't buy $7,000 worth of unspecified guiding services. When a guide and outfitter charges a big league fee, he had better be prepared to provide big league service!

If I could only hunt one species of game for the rest of my life, it would be bears. For variety, for availability, for sheer excitement—they just can't be beat!

2

Where to Hunt in the U.S. and Canada

BLACK BEARS

Twenty-nine states and most Canadian provinces have a black bear season. Obviously some offer better hunting than others.

Let's eliminate Texas right now. No bears have been killed there in modern times—because there are no bears to kill—so I don't understand why they continue to offer a season. It sounds like one of those unholy regulations that was set by a politician rather than a wildlife biologist!

In Alaska the best area is in the southern coastal sections. Blacks and grizzlies don't mix very well so it is usually tough to double up hunt these two species. However, in Alaska anything is possible. Game Management Units 1, 2, and 6 are good sections. The annual average harvest is around 4,000; with so much other game in the state, blacks are still considered to be vermin by most resident hunters.

Nonresident hunters are not required to have a guide, but due to

7

the complexity of the game regulations and necessity of ground transportation, it is a good idea to book one. Spring black bear hunts in southeastern Alaska are very economical and can be planned to coincide with some excellent fishing. In some areas you can even take two bears. For more information write Alaska Department of Fish & Game, Subport Building, Juneau, Alaska 99801.

Arizona black bear populations seem to be greater than earlier estimates. This state has certainly produced its share of trophy-class bears in recent years. Best bets would have to include the Indian reservations and counties mentioned in the chapter on trophy bears (chapter 17). Arizona only has a fall season. For more information write Arizona Game and Fish Department, 2222 West Greenway Road, Phoenix, Arizona 85023.

Arkansas' first bear season in fifty-three years was opened in December 1980. The state started a vigorous stocking program in the 1960s which was responsible for the reestablishment of huntable bear populations in a state that was formerly nicknamed "The Black Bear State." Still, there are better places to go than Arkansas if you are a nonresident hunter planning a trip. Resident hunters should certainly begin to develop bear hunting skills and begin scouting for sign near abundant acorn crops and rock outcroppings which the bears seem to frequent. Game Zones 2, 5, and 11 have the densest populations at this time. For more information write Arkansas Game & Fish Commission, No. 2 Natural Resources Drive, Little Rock, Arkansas 72205.

Northern California has to rank somewhere near the top in locales. Pursuing bears with hounds in the mountains of northern California is just about all the excitement and grandeur any hunter can stand. Your chances of bagging a "bragging size" bruin there is certainly above average compared to most other parts of the U.S. For more information contact Shasta-Cascade Wonderland Association, PO Box 1988, Redding, California 96099, or California Department of Fish & Game, 1416 Ninth Street, Sacramento, California 95814.

In Colorado you can hunt bears over baits and with dogs in both spring and fall. It is hard not to find some sort of bear hunting to your liking in this Rocky Mountain state. There is some decent black bear hunting just about anywhere in the Colorado Rockies, with the best areas being in the southern part of the state in Archuleta County. The San Juan National Forest and the country around the Arkansas River aren't too shabby either. For information write Colorado Division of Wildlife, 6060 Broadway, Denver, Colorado 80216.

Florida allows hunting with dogs. Best bets are in the panhandle in the Apalachicola National Forest and in the central part of the state in the Ocala National Forest. The season is broken up and all areas are not open all the time, so check current regulations when planning your hunt. For more information write Florida Game and Fresh Water Fish Commission, 620 South Meridian Street, Tallahassee, Florida 32301.

Georgia only allows hunting on selected wildlife management areas during segments of the deer season. No hounds or bait are allowed. The bear habitat is steep rugged terrain in the Southern Appalachians. Bear seasons are shifted about among the wildlife management areas (wma's) each year so you will have to check current regulations. Rich Mountain, Cohutta, and Coopers Creek wma's are good places to try. For more information write Georgia Department of Natural Resources, Game and Fish Division, 270 Washington Street, Atlanta, Georgia 30334.

Idaho currently allows hunters to take two bears since populations are at a cyclic peak. Many guides in Idaho offer hound hunts for lion and bear and have pretty high success ratios. Baits and hounds are allowed in some areas. For more information write Idaho Department of Fish and Game, PO Box 25, Boise, Idaho 83707.

Louisiana is another one of the southeastern states that is enjoying an increase in black bear populations due to sound bear management. The bears in Louisiana have just recently reached huntable populations, and seasons are short to prevent overhunting. For more information write Louisiana Department of Wildlife and Fisheries, 400 Royal Street, New Orleans, Louisiana 70130.

Maine is considered to be one of the better black bear hunting states and deservedly so; it has one of the best bear populations in the East. Bears were considered vermin by most residents until just a few years ago, when they discovered nonresident hunters would be attracted to the state by good bear hunting opportunities. They recently closed the spring season to afford additional refuge for this valuable resource. For information write Maine Department of Inland Fisheries and Wildlife, 284 State Street, Station No. 41, Augusta, Maine 04333.

You can hunt bears in Massachusetts, but it is hardly worth the effort since the statewide annual kill only averages about ten bears per season. For more information write Division of Fisheries and Wildlife, 100 Cambridge Street, Boston, Massachusetts 02202.

You can hunt bears over bait and with hounds in Michigan, and you have a pretty fair chance of bagging a bruin since hunters average about nine hundred bears per year. Best areas are in the far north-western section of the upper peninsula. For more details write Wildlife Division, Michigan Department of Natural Resources, Lansing, Michigan 48909.

In Minnesota you can hunt over baits but not with hounds. Officials decided to drop the fall bear season, held during the regular deer season, and the kill dropped from around 1,000 to 743. The best counties are St. Louis, Itasca, Lake, Aitkin, Cass and Cook. For more information contact Minnesota Department of Natural Resources, Central Building, St. Paul, Minnesota 55112.

Montana's black bear season is usually open at the same time as elk, deer, and grizzly, making it possible for a hunter to take several species in the same general area. No baits or hounds are allowed, so more bears are taken by accident rather than design while hunters go after elk and deer. For more information write Montana Fish, Wildlife, and Parks, 1420 East Sixth Avenue, Helena, Montana 56901.

In New Hampshire you can hunt bears over bait, with dogs, or by still hunting. Biologists have kept data on how bears are taken and it is rather startling; only two or three percent are taken over baits, twenty-five percent are taken with dogs, and forty to sixty percent are taken by still hunters during the deer season. Coos, Grafton and Carroll Counties account for the annual average bear kill of approximately two hundred. For more information write New Hampshire Fish & Game Department, 34 Bridge Street, Concord, New Hampshire 03331.

Bear seasons in New Mexico are usually concurrent with other fall big game seasons. Baiting is not allowed. Hounds are only permitted prior to the opening of other big game seasons. Regulations are based on a complex system of hunting regions, so get a copy of current regulations from New Mexico Department of Game and Fish, Villagra Building, Santa Fe, New Mexico 87503.

The Adirondack and Catskill Mountains of New York provide some excellent bear habitat and consequently some outstanding bear hunting. The regular season usually coincides with deer season, which accounts for the majority of bears being killed by hunters on stand waiting for their winter supply of venison. Weather conditions determine to a great degree the success of such hunts. If bad weather sets in before the seasons open, the bears will be denned up and not very active. The best hunting is in the Adirondacks and includes Franklin, Hamilton, and Essex counties. For more information write Department of Environmental Conservation, 50 Wolf Road, Albany, New York 12233.

Bear hunting in North Carolina is concentrated in the western mountains and eastern swamps and is generally a social affair consisting of ten to twenty-five hunters. The hardiest of the bunch follow the dogs through some of the roughest and steepest terrain in North America. (Pay attention: this is the voice of experience speaking.) Other members of the group are stationed at strategic locations in hopes of bagging a bear at a "crossing," which usually consists of a gap between two high peaks or on some well-used game trail. Guiding in North Carolina consists mostly of letting paying clients join one of the hunting parties. You won't be pampered and waited on on one of these hunts, but it will be an experience you'll never forget. For more information write North Carolina Wildlife Resources, Division of Game, 512 North Salisbury Street, Raleigh, North Carolina 27611.

Most of Oregon's better black bear hunting sections lie in the northeast corner and along the coastal counties. Both bait and hounds are legal, and there are many guides and outfitters who cater to bear hunters. For information write Department of Fish and Wildlife, 506 S.W. Mill Street, Portland, Oregon 97208.

To say that bear hunting enthusiasm in Pennsylvania has escalated in recent years is a gross understatement. In just three years—from 1973 to 1976—the number of bear hunters leaped from less than 100,000 to over 200,000, and that was for a one day season! On December 17, 1979 alone, 736 black bears were harvested by hunters. One hundred sixty-six were taken in a single hour! Back in 1924 it took hunters an entire fifty-four-day season to bag 924. Some of the best hunting areas in the Keystone State are Lycoming, Clinton, and Pike Counties. Also prime bear territory are the swampy valleys of the Pocono Mountains— just 90 miles from The Big Apple! For more information write Pennsylvania Game Commission, PO Box 1567, Harrisburg, Pennsylvania 17120.

The bear take in South Carolina is sparse, running somewhere around half a dozen a year. All the hunting is concentrated in Pickens County, where they are hunted with dogs. For more information write South Carolina Wildlife and Marine Resources, PO Box 167, Columbia, South Carolina 20209.

Most of Tennessee's best bear hunting is in those counties which border the Great Smoky Mountains National Park. These counties are located in the extreme eastern end of the state along the North Carolina border. For information write Tennessee Wildlife Resources Agency, PO Box 40747, Nashville, Tennessee 37204.

Utah is not the best Rocky Mountain bear hunting state. The average annual kill is only around thirty-five animals. Hounds are legal, but only bowhunters can hunt over a bait. The best bet is to hire a guide who has a good pack of hounds. For more information write Utah Division of Wildlife Resources, 1596 West North Temple, Salt Lake City, Utah 84116.

In Vermont the bear season traditionally runs during the middle part of the deer season, and most bears are taken by deer hunters who accidentally encounter them. Baits aren't allowed, but hounds are. The average annual kill varies but has averaged around two hundred fifty for the last decade. Considering the size of the state, Vermont has a very respectable bear population, due primarily to lots of good habitat. For more information write Vermont Fish and Game Department, State Office Building, Montpeiler, Vermont 05602.

Virginia has to be ranked among the top three among the southern bear states based upon an estimated population of between 1,000 and 1,500 statewide and an annual kill. Best hunting is in the George Washington and Jefferson national forests. The highest annual kill for the past decade was 432, registered in 1981. Baits are not allowed, but hounds are, with some restrictions. For more information write Virginia Commission on Game and Inland Fisheries, PO Box 1104, Richmond, Virginia 23230.

Washington has the best bear hunting of all the contiguous states based on population estimates and annual harvest. The population is estimated at a whopping 29,000 with a rather considerable harvest of about 3,000 per year. Nearly one out of every three bears killed in the lower forty-eight states come from Washington. For more information write Washington Game Department, 600 North Capitol Way, Olympia, Washington 98504.

The best bets in West Virginia bear would include Pocahontas, Greenbrier, and Randolph counties. Hounds, but not baits, are allowed. Annual harvests average between forty and fifty. For additional information write Department of Natural Resources, 1800 Washington Street East, Charleston, West Virginia 25305.

Wisconsin has one of the best bear populations in the Midwest, with the best hunting to be had in the northernmost counties, along the Michigan border. The state reported its largest annual harvest in 1981 of 1,243 bears, with 59 percent being taken with bait, 34 percent with dogs, and seven percent by all other methods. For more information write Wisconsin Department of Natural Resources, PO Box 7921, Madison, Wisconsin 53707.

Wyoming, according to figures from the National Rifle Association, has the highest hunter success figures on black bear of any state—a whopping 27.5 percent. Baiting is legal for both spring and fall hunts, with many guides and outfitters catering to bear hunters. Teton and Sublette counties are traditional high success areas. For more information contact Wyoming Game and Fish Department, Cheyenne, Wyoming 82002.

Ontario probably has the highest black bear population of all states and provinces. It would be hard to find a region that didn't offer some dandy bear hunting. I hunt Ontario regularly. In fact, I collected a bear last spring, and I already have both a spring and fall hunt booked this year! The province has an abundance of excellent guides and outfitters who cater to bear hunters. For more information write Ontario Travel, Hearst Block, Queen's Park, Toronto, Ontario, Canada M7A2E5.

Quebec is another eastern Canadian province which offers some outstanding black bear hunting, with both spring and fall hunts. Baits and hounds are legal. For more information write Gouvernment du Quebec, Ministere du Loisir de la Chasse et de la Peche, Direction des communications, Case postale 22 000, Quebec, Canada G1K 7X2.

There is excellent black bear hunting in southern British Columbia, with spring and fall hunting. Bait is not legal but you can use hounds. The best pelts are usually taken during the April to June spring hunting season. For an extra trophy fee you can take a second bear. It is one of the few areas I know where you stand a good chance of taking both a cinnamon-colored and a black pelt in the same area. For more information write Province of British Columbia, Ministry of Environment, Victoria, British Columbia, Canada.

The best bear hunting in Saskatchewan lies in the northern two-thirds of the province where there is wooded habitat. Black bear hunting is probably not as good as in the western or eastern provinces, but it still affords outstanding possibilities by most standards. For more information write Saskatchewan Tourism and Renewable Resources, 3211 Albert Street, Regina, Saskatchewan, Canada S4S 5W6.

It is hard to pinpoint best bet areas in Alberta. Those areas north of Edmonton and along the British Columbia border are just about as good as you will find anywhere. The best estimates on annual black bear harvest range around 4,000 per year. No baits or hounds are allowed. For additional information write Energy and Natural Resources, Fish and Wildlife Division, 9915 108th Street, Edmonton, Alberta, Canada T5K 2C9.

New Brunswick averages about 600 black bear kills a year, with residents accounting for about twenty percent and nonresidents about thirty-five percent. Both spring and fall hunts are offered. Bears are fairly well distributed throughout the province, with the best areas being those where guides and outfitters are available such as York, Victoria, and Carlton counties. For more information contact Department of Natural Resources, Fish and Wildlife Branch, PO Box 6000, Frederiction, New Brunswick, Canada E3B 5H1.

Black bear population estimates range from 15,000 to 30,000 in Manitoba. There is better than average bear hunting just about anywhere in the province excepting the farm regions of the Southwest. No hounds are allowed, but baiting is legal. Nonresidents are required to have a guide. For more information contact Department of Natural Resources, Fish and Wildlife Branch, 1495 St. James Street, Box 22, Winnipeg, Manitoba, Canada R3H 0W9.

Newfoundland hardly ranks as a prime bear hunting province since the annual kill is less than a hundred. Some efforts are underway to improve the situation.

Nova Scotia records an average annual black bear harvest of approximately four hundred. The four western counties of Shel-burne, Annapolis, Queens, and Yarmouth are high success areas. A guide is required for bear hunting. For more information contact Department of Lands and Forests, PO Box 698, Halifax, Nova Scotia, Canada B3J 2T9.

The Northwest Territories offer scant black bear hunting opportunities for the nonresident hunter. Nonresidents are restricted to a very small area and must have a Class A guide to hunt. If you want to hunt bear, grizzly or polar bears would be better choices considering the cost of the hunt. For more information contact Department of Renewable Resources, Yellowknife, Northwest Territories, Canada X1A 2L9.

In the Yukon the low annual kill figures of 150 black bears are not indicative of the black bear hunting potential there; most hunters are after grizzly. The blacks in the Yukon sport long, luxuriant pelts, and you should have many animals to choose from. For more information write Department of Renewable Resources, Wildlife Branch, Box 2703, Whitehorse, Yukon Territory, Canada Y1A 2C6.

After all those tidbits, a few "bottom lines" of summary are in order. Your best bets, based on populations and hunter success ratios, would be Washington, Ontario, British Columbia, Alaska, Idaho, Oregon, and Montana. You could put all those names in a hat and I wouldn't really care which one I drew for a black bear hunt.

GRIZZLY

Unless you are a resident of Montana or Alaska or a Canadian province which allows resident grizzly hunting, you will have to have a guide on any grizzly hunt you make. Grizzly hunts for those who are not residents in grizzly country are expensive, ranging from a marginal $3,500 to over $7,000. And those figures do not include travel—just guides and licenses! For most hunters, a grizzly hunt is a once in a lifetime proposition. Even a wealthy sportsman cannot afford to enter into a hunt for griz without careful analysis of all prospective choices.

Let's get Montana out of the way first since it offers the least opportunity for a serious grizzly hunter. Each year the state issues a total of 500 grizzly permits which are good only in certain areas. If I was hunting for other species in one of these areas, I would purchase the $150 griz license on the chance I would get a shot while after other species. I would not book a guided hunt in Montana for the sole purpose of taking a grizzly. When the annual quota of twenty-five bears is reached, the season is promptly closed.

Alaska offers some good prospects for grizzly, and many guides offer special bear hunts. Much of Alaska's prime grizzly range was declared off limits by President Carter's establishment of 56 million acres as national monuments. These monuments were established to protect Alaskan wilderness from bulldozers and oil prospecting. What it did, in effect, was concentrate all the bear, moose, and sheep hunters into a much smaller area and put a lot of stress on the areas left open. When the president decreased the available hunting land, he also decreased the available supply of territory guides could utilize, and consequently the demand caused a considerable bump in the cost of an Alaskan trip. I could book a hunt right now for Cape buffalo in Zambia that would cost me $3,500 round trip from New York. An Alaska grizzly hunt could easily run twice that amount. For all practical purposes, the average hunter in the middle income bracket is effectively priced out of any chance of ever going grizzly hunting. But although the cost is prohibitively high, there is still some good grizzly hunting for those who have the big bucks to pay the tab.

The Talkeetna Range in Alaska was open for spring grizzly hunts in 1981 for the first time in twenty years. It should offer some opportunities for the light-colored "toklat" color phase of the mountain grizzly.

The Copper River Basin is another area where grizzlies prosper. The Alaska Range and Brooks Range have some good hunting if you can book a hunt in an area that is open to sport hunting.

Grizzly populations in Alaska are at an all time high, certainly for this century. But the big bear's future is uncertain as more and more people move into the remote wilderness habitat—a habitat that is necessary if the grizzly is to survive in huntable numbers. Some biologists feel that controlled sport hunting even aids in producing stable grizzly populations since hunters prefer to take the big mature bears, increasing the survival rate of immature boars. An old boar won't tolerate the presence of a young male, and they can inflict terrible damage on the youngsters.

British Columbia has some excellent grizzly hunting, especially in the northern section and around Bella Coola. If you doubt the capability of the Bella Coola region to produce record grizzlies, then just look in the Boone & Crockett book. Most hunters book what is referred to as a combination hunt, and grizzlies are usually on the list of possible trophies along with sheep and moose.

If you really had your heart set on a trophy-class grizzly, then I would suggest that you book at least a ten-day hunt and have your guide understand up front that a big grizzly was your first priority. After you get your grizzly, then you can worry about the other stuff on the list.

There is some prime grizzly hunting to be had in the Yukon Territory also. Biologists estimate that there are somewhere between 6,000 and 10,000 grizzlies scattered between the southern border and the coast of the Arctic Ocean.

Rivers and flood plains attract grizzlies in the spring when they first come out of their dens and are on the prowl for carrion, roots, and grasses. Then the river bottom activity drops off until the soap berries begin to ripen in early July. Another prime time for grizzlies along the stream side trails is when the salmon are spawning. Yet another choice location is on one of the big open "slides" where a winter snow slide has wiped away all the trees and underbrush. These areas are usually the first place where grass sprouts in the spring, and since grass is the prime component of a grizzly's spring menu, these two just go together. Stay on the downwind side and glass them with binoculars. A spotting scope also comes in handy for evaluating potential trophies from a distance.

Alberta doesn't have as large a grizzly population as Alaska, British Columbia, or the Yukon, but they do have about fifteen hundred running around within their borders. Alberta's grizzlies are not as widely dispersed as those the Yukon, so there are "pockets" of fairly decent hunting.

BROWN BEAR

Kodiak Island and the Alaskan Peninsula are the prime areas for really big brown bear. They are also the best areas to pick up a really big tab for your hunt. Brown bear hunts further south may not produce as many record class browns—they are pretty scarce even up north—but the area still turns up a record bear occasionally.

You can hunt from a boat that cruises the coastline until a bear is spotted, and then you go ashore for a stalk and the shot. If the salmon are spawning, then you and your guide can ease along a salmon stream until you have a social encounter with a brown.

A ten-day hunt from a boat will run about $3,500 or higher by the time you read this. There are also some hunts being offered by boat on the Kenai River southeast of Anchorage.

POLAR BEAR

It won't take long to summarize the polar bear hunting situation. You can only hunt them in the Northwest Territories, and it will cost you $15,000 in Canadian funds or about $12,000 at the current rate of exchange. You cannot bring the pelt into the U.S. since polar bears are classified as a threatened species. I have a friend who arranges polar bear hunts, and he fills his quota of twelve hunters every year. Last year they were 100 percent successful.

A polar bear hunt is extremely expensive and requires enormous determination and resolve to travel on the ice pack by dogsled; yet it is probably one of the last great adventures on this planet. (Photo courtesy of Travel Manitoba)

These are traditional hunts where you go out onto the ice by dog sled and stalk Nanook on the ice. This is probably one of the last sho-nuff-go-to-hell adventures left on the face of our overdeveloped, overpopulated, and overpolluted planet. The only problem is—you have to be as rich as an Arab sheik to pay the freight!

I have purposely avoided being specific about season dates, license fees, and bag limits as these tend to be in a state of constant flux while states and provinces intensify bear research and bear management techniques. (I have in hand all the current regulations and fees for the 1982 seasons, but these would be obsolete by the time this book hits the shelves.) Rather than give current fees and dates, I have provided instead the addresses of each state and province which has a bear season so that you can write for the most current regulations. These sources, in most cases, will provide a list of registered guides upon request.

I usually keep pretty up-to-date on guides and outfitters who specialize in bear hunting. If I can be of assistance in helping you plan a bear hunt, write to me, Jerry Meyer, at Route 1, Talking Rock, Georgia 30175.

3

Bears: Their Natural History, Habitat, and Habits

BLACK BEAR

The ubiquituous black bear, *Ursus americanus,* is native to just about all of North America excluding the plains of the Midwest and the southern parts of the Pacific coast. This adaptable creature is as at home in the Canadian Rockies as he is in the swamps of central Florida. It is estimated that in primitive times 500,000 black bears roamed on this continent. The best guesstimate of current populations puts the total number just shy of half that number.

Although found in a wide variety of dissimilar habitats, black bears seem to prefer and thrive best in mixed coniferous-decidous forests.

A black bear is not always black but can range in color from black to a metallic blue. Black is the most common color for the species with the cinnamon phase of the Rocky Mountain bears running second. The blue glacier or Kermode phase found in Alaska is extremely rare. Some bears in the Rockies appear almost blond!

The black bear is more numerous than people realize. Recent bear research indicates that there are more bears in the woods than even the research biologists thought were possible.

A mature black bear will stand between three and four feet at the shoulder. The average weight for a mature adult will range from 200 to 300 pounds depending upon time of the year and quality of the food source. There can be a difference of a hundred pounds or more in a bear's weight when he emerges from the den in the spring and when he is fattened up in late fall prior to going back into the den. There have been a few bears that reached the exceptional weight of over 600 pounds!

The profile of a black bear's face is rather strange, with a slightly Roman nose, as opposed to the dished-out profile of a grizzly. This difference in facial profile is one of the basic methods of distinguishing a grizzly from the brown phase of the black bear. A grizzly also has a noticeable hump on top of his shoulders. I studied these anatomical differences with considerable concentration prior to my first trip into grizzly country so I would be able to tell the difference.

The first grizzly I ever saw was in Alaska—and believe me, I knew he was a griz the moment I saw him feeding on a slope 300 yards away. One look through my binoculars told me I was looking at my first grizzly. I didn't need to check the shape of his nose or look for a hump on his back—he just looked infinitely more ferocious than any black bear I had ever seen. This difference in the species may not be as obvious to someone who hasn't looked at a lot of black bears. Then they will all probably look like grizzlies, in which case the nose and back silhouette differences will be helpful in distinguishing between the two.

Mating season for bears ranges from June to July depending upon their location, with the later dates being more common in the more northern regions. The cubs, ranging in number from one to five with two being the average, are born the following January or February while the mother is still in the winter den. The cubs are six to eight inches long at birth and weigh just about ten ounces! This is only about one two-hundredth of the mother's weight.

A cub will increase his weight from forty to sixty pounds in his first year. Males continue to grow for about seven years, with females stopping their growth somewhat earlier. Usually males and females reach sexual maturity between their third and fourth year, but it may not occur until the seventh year in some locales.

Bears do not hibernate in the true sense of the word, but rather are in a deep sleep from which they can be aroused. The winter of 1982–83 was exceptionally mild in the Great Smoky Mountains National Park and Dr. Mike Pelton told me that the warm weather had produced some strange denning patterns, with the bears leaving their dens more often than usual and seemingly sleeping lighter when in the den.

Research into the deep sleep and slowed metabolism of bears is the focus of considerable research in hopes that a similar sleep may be induced in astronauts on long space flights.

Bears emerge from their dens in the spring, which is April for my bruin neighbors here around my home in the southern Appalachian Mountains, but may be as late as the last of May for more northern climes.

Bears, especially the males, are habitual wanderers. They will tend to stay in a prescribed territory but may wander over twenty miles in a day's time. Some wander on a circuit that may take three days to complete. Bears that have been live trapped and transported fifty miles while under anesthesia have returned to their original territory in two days to be caught again in the same campground pilfering campers' groceries! In some areas a bear's summer range may only be about six square miles, while the fall range may be more than fifteen square miles.

The black bear has a considerable vocal repertoire of growls, roars, sniffs, woofs, and an unnerving pop-pop-pop made by snapping his jaws. I once observed a boar in the Smokies making determined advances on a sow with reproduction on his mind. The lady was not so inclined to such a relationship and said so in no uncertain terms by popping her jaws. It was an awesome primordial sound that soon turned that boar's amorous intentions to a sudden urge to travel in search of more submissive companionship!

The sounds emitted by young cubs are not unlike the cries and squalls of a human infant. John Long once introduced me to a lady who was fishing with her husband for walleyes on the Ghoast River in northern Ontario when she heard what she thought was a small child crying "Help! Help!" She investigated and found a small bear cub clinging to the limb of a tree that had fallen into the river. She was so convinced the cry was coming from a human infant that she thought she had found a small Negro child until she got close enough to see it was a bear cub.

Bears are truly omnivorous, with vegetable matter making up the biggest majority of their diet during most of the year. They also feed heavily on fish or winter-killed carion when it is available. They will also kill deer, sheep or other medium sized mammals when the opportunity presents itself or hunger requires it.

Bears are devoted diggers of insects, grubs and rodents. They will also turn over every rock along a stream while looking for salamanders. Their affection for beehives is well known, and they eat honey, larvae, adults, and comb with equal relish.

They also feed on a wide variety of nuts and fruits as they are available. Bears will climb an oak tree and break out the upper limbs to get at acorns that are not mature enough to fall to the ground. They will use the same tactic of breaking down the limbs of apple trees so they can stand on the ground and feed on the fruit more easily.

Hunters have long recognized the wisdom of keeping a watch over blueberry patches when the berries are ripe and plentiful and bears feed on them almost exclusively.

Cubs usually stay with their mothers until the breeding season of their second year. At that time, the adolescents are chased off to search for their own territory. These year-and-a-half-old cubs are usually the ones responsible for the numerous stories of bears showing up in towns. These inexperienced bears are notorious wanderers and many meet unfortunate ends when they wander into suburbia.

Bears have lived for twenty-five to thirty years in captivity, but it is estimated that most wild bears are less than ten years old.

Black bears are able and willing tree climbers and can climb trees all of their lives. Grizzlies, on the other hand, are not good climbers because of their long claws. I once heard that one way to tell if you were being chased by a grizzly or a black was to climb a tree. If he followed you up the tree and ate you, it was a black bear. If he pulled the tree up by the roots, shook you out and then ate you, it was a grizzly!

GRIZZLIES

Taxonomists have in recent years endowed the grizzly and the brown bear with the same scientific name—*Ursus arctos*. The current thinking is that they are both the same species and differ only in size due to the more favorable and abundant food supply of the Alaska coastline where the larger browns reside. I thought the old scientific name of the grizzly, *Ursus horribilis*, which loosely translates into "horrible bear," was more appropriate!

Next to a riled leopard, a riled grizzly is probably the most deadly and most ferocious animal on this planet. His agility and grim determination are what make him so deadly when aroused.

A big grizzly can go up to 800 pounds and stand nearly four feet at the top of the hump on his shoulders. Grizzly cubs can climb trees but the nearly four-inch claws of the adult prevent such agility.

Grizzlies come in a wide range of colors including dark brown, yellowish brown, or almost blond. The hair on a mature grizzly will often be silver tipped, which accounts for the nicknames of "silvertip" and "grizzly." The grizzly of the Rocky Mountains was referred to by members of the Lewis and Clark expedition as the "white bear" because of the whitish hue of the sun shining on the silver-tipped hair.

The greatest portion of grizzlies live in Alaska, British Columbia, the Yukon and the Northwest Territories. There is only a token, and

A typical silver-tipped grizzly displaying the prominent hump at the shoulders and the dished-out facial profile. (Photo by R.J. Hayes)

apparently endangered, population in Glacier National Park and Yellowstone National Park.

Grizzlies usually mate in late May and June, with the young born the following January. The cubs range in number from two to four, are about nine inches long, and weigh up to one and one-half pounds. By the time the mother leaves the den in late April or early May, the cubs are able to tag along after their mother. They have begun to eat solid food but will continue to nurse until fall.

Grizzlies are omnivorous and feed mostly on vegetation but show a decided preference for carion, salmon, and fresh meat when it can be obtained. I once watched a grizzly in Alaska spend hours digging for marmots on a hillside. The long claws are well adapted to digging and it seemed like that grizzly was moving a ton of dirt to get to a small morsel that may have weighed a pound and a half.

In summer and fall, grizzlies converge on salmon streams and dine heavily on spawning salmon. Contrary to popular belief, they don't swat the salmon up on shore, as depicted in many drawings; rather, they thrust their head into the water and grab the fish in their teeth.

In spite of its massive size, the grizzly is extremely agile and is capable of speeds up to thirty-five miles per hour when charging. Thirty-five miles per hour may not sound very fast, until a grizzly is traveling at that speed at close range in your direction! A grizzly attains this speed in about two jumps and can travel this fast through alder thickets, over steep slopes, and across rocky ground where a hunter can barely walk. This rapid acceleration allows a grizzly to catch and kill prey and hunters before either has much chance for escape or defense, especially if the charge is initiated from close range.

Sexual maturity varies between four and eight years, with the males usually maturing at an earlier age. Grizzlies practice a rather rigid form of social hierarchy based upon such factors as age, size, and sex determining dominance. This practice reduces somewhat the fierce physical encounters which occur during mating.

As a general rule, grizzlies are solitary animals that establish a range and defend it against other bears. There are two exceptions to this rule: one, if the griz is a female with cubs under the age of two, and two, if it is a season when salmon are spawning and the bears are attracted to this abundant food source. Dominant bears will establish their own stretch of fishing water and chase off any intruders. This practice may be responsible for some of the grizzly-man confrontations which occur along salmon streams. The thick brush along most salmon rivers, the noise of the rushing water, and the intense concentration of a fishing bear are all conducive to a bear and a man suddenly coming face to face without either one knowing the other was anywhere around. Beware: A surprised bear is a dangerous bear!

Like many wild animals, the survival of the grizzly is directly related to the destruction of habitat, except he is more affected. A grizzly may require a home range of just over one hundred square miles that must include such components as food sources (like salmon streams, moose, deer, or other large prey), winter den sites, summer ranges, grazing areas, digging sites, and mating sites, to name a few. This area must also be relatively free of man and his livestock.

When men and grizzlies have frequent contacts, the inevitable conflict will arise, with fatal results to one of the participants. If we are to have griz in the lower forty-eight, then we must establish game refuges where the rights and needs of this great beast are paramount. Such a refuge would have no public campgrounds, condominiums or other "improvements" and could not be leased to cattlemen for grazing, nor to mining companies for exploration. The sole and absolute function of the region would be the perpetuation of grizzlies—period!

If this proposal sounds too extreme, let me inform you that, in tiny Japan, where every available square foot is cultivated to feed its dense human population, there are more grizzlies than in the lower forty-eight states! It is just a matter of priorities. We can have *real* grizzly habitat, or we can have a bastardized Disney World for campers and call it another "national park." I am not opposed to having the plastic wilderness areas where millions of people go camping each year. For those who equate "tent slums" with an outdoor experience, I support their right to have such places to enjoy. But I also believe that there should be a few areas where grizzlies can be "lord of their domain" because that is all a grizzly knows how to be!

POLAR BEARS

The range of the polar bear (*Ursus maritimus*) is circumpolar and in Canada consists of the permanent ice pack of the Arctic Ocean southward to James Bay. Polar bears tend to be nomads and may be found throughout their range. But they tend to spend time in certain areas, based on seasonal needs) breeding, denning, feeding, and retreating.

Only the females den up for extended periods of time, usually from early November to late March. The cubs are born in this den and usually emerge with the mother in April, spending a few days near the "maternity den" before accompanying the mother out onto the sea ice to hunt for ringed and bearded seals, the primary food of polar bears. (They also will occasionally eat walrus, beluga whales, sea birds, and kelp.)

As the ice melts in summer, polar bears either move northward with the retreating ice or move onto land where they lounge around in any remaining snow banks. With the formation of autumn ice, the bears move back onto the ice for their primary occupation of hunting seals.

The incidence of polar bear–man confrontations has been on the increase during recent years. In 1977-78, there were ten defense or nuisance kills; 1978-79, 16 kills; 1979-80, 34 kills; and 1980-81, 24 kills. Some circumstances suggest that a fatal attack on a human was triggered because the man was behaving in a way that caused the polar

Despite being on the endangered species list, the great white polar bear has shown an increase in population in recent years. (Photo courtesy of Canada North Outfitters)

bear to think he was a seal. As more and more mineral exploration and oil production activities take place on or near the arctic ice pack, more man–polar bear encounters can be anticipated.

An extensive program of polar bear detection and deterrent research is currently underway at Cape Churchill, Manitoba, and in the Northwest Territories. In recent years, polar bears have been coming ashore along the northern Manitoba and Ontario coasts when ice melts in Hudson Bay. The bears move northward along the coast and congregate in large numbers at Cape Churchill during September and November. As the ice freezes in mid-November, they disperse out onto the ice to hunt seals.

While this dense population of polar bears is residing on the cape, many spectators gather to observe and photograph the bears. Obviously this concentration of bears and humans leads to some very interesting and exciting confrontations. In an effort to reduce these encounters, a wide variety of techniques have been devised. Recordings of barking dogs did not stop the advance of 87 percent of the bears and, in four instances, elicited aggressive responses. A 38mm riot gun firing rubber projectiles successfully deterred all the bears it was used on. The bears darted with an antibiotic left the study area, and 93 percent of the bears tested passed through the electric fence.

It is difficult to accurately assess the population trends of polar bears due to their nomadic life styles and, in some areas, the small sample population studied. It will require some long-range population studies to determine major population trends and the effect of such events as oil spills, human-bear encounters, and other influences on the bear's Arctic habitat.

4

Planning and Preparing for a Bear Hunt

There is a lot more to planning and preparing for a bear hunt than just grabbing a rifle and a handful of shells and heading to the woods. Especially if you are going on a once-in-a-lifetime hunt for grizzly, brown, or polar bear. If you are going after one of these "big three," you can expect to spend somewhere between $5,000 and $15,000. (A black bear hunt runs from $400 to $1,000.) Even if you have the big bucks to go after a glamour bear, you may still be limited to a once-in-a-lifetime experience because some provinces only allow you to take one brown or grizzly in your lifetime. I expect this trend to become more widespread in the future, and I am not so sure it is such a bad idea.

For many sportsmen, the price of taking a brown ($6,000), grizzly ($5,000), or polar bear ($12,000) is already out of reach. There are those who save for years to make what is literally the hunt of a lifetime, only to experience bitter disappointment when that dream hunt is a nightmare. However, the disappointment is not always the fault of the outfitter.

The above rates are average guided brown or grizzly bear hunts to give you some idea about the current costs, which are certainly subject to change. Some hunts include trophy fees and licenses; others do not. You need to have in writing just exactly what your guide costs include and also any additional expenses that will be added later.

As an example, I once had a hunter tell me about an outfitter who sold him a hunt that was "all inclusive" except for taxidermy and trophy fees. After he got a nice bear the outfitter tacked on a $200 taxidermy fee for skinning the bear and another $50 for shipping the hide to a taxidermist who charged an outrageous fee that included a kickback to the outfitter. He also charged a $200 trophy fee which did not include the fee he had to pay to the province where he hunted. He got almost $500 bucks in "surprise sucker" fees tacked onto what he thought was "an all inclusive single price hunt." I cannot emphasize too much the importance of getting everything in writing, spelling out specifically what you pay and what you get for your money.

The first step in planning any big bucks big game hunt is to do a lot of research. Compile a list of all the guides and outfitters who specialize in the species you are after. There are guides who will offer you several species in a single hunt, but you will have to establish some priorities on even one of these multiple hunts. Don't expect to spend seven days in the bush and collect goat, sheep, moose, and grizzly!

Search the ads in outdoor magazines. Write to the game and fish departments in the states and provinces that have open season on the species you are interested in. Ask them for information on licenses, game populations, kill figures, hunter success figures and trends in populations; ask for some suggestions on the best places to hunt; and ask for a list of licensed guides and outfitters.

Collect as much information and as many names and addresses of guides as you can. Once you have compiled your list, write each one asking for information on fees, services provided, any guarantees, best times to come, equipment provided, and most important of all, a list of *recent* clients. Ask for the names and addresses of both successful and unsuccessful clients. If an outfitter sends you copies of letters from satisfied clients, contact them—the letters may have been typed by his mother-in-law! Seriously, the most important thing you can do when it comes to selecting an outfitter or guide who is going to charge you several thousand bucks for a hunt is to check on each and every reference he sends you. You wouldn't buy a five thousand-dollar diamond, waterfront lot, car, or horse from some guy just because you saw an ad in a magazine, would you? To book a five thousand-dollar hunt without checking on the outfitter and the quality of his hunts is just as foolish!

I do not mean to imply that all guides and outfitters are shysters. Most of them are honorable men who give you your money's worth. But with the cost of guided hunts skyrocketing, the big bucks are attracting some folks who are after quick, easy money.

Don't be bashful about asking a guide for references and about the services he provides. You will be spending a lot of money, and the reputable guides do not mind providing you with the information you request. If you get in touch with an outfitter who seems to resent your requests for information and references, forget him!

Don't expect to locate a good guide and go grizzly hunting in a month. Most of the guides who are worth anything stay booked up for a year or more. This is especially true of the guides who specialize in the "big three." A year to a year and a half is a reasonable time for planning and booking a hunt. (I actually enjoy the anticipation of planning and preparing for a special hunt that is a year or so away.)

Once the date is set and the guide is booked, then you have to make sure that you don't louse up your own dream hunt. Collect the equipment you will use, the clothing you will wear, the gun you will shoot and the boots you will wear.

(Years ago, when I was fresh out of college and struggling to raise a family on my salary as a professional staff member of the Boy Scouts of America, I was in a gun store in Atlanta looking and wishing. While I was there, two guys in polyester suits came in to buy grizzly rifles. They were leaving for Alaska the next Saturday and didn't even own a gun. They just decided to go shoot a grizzly, and they had the bucks to pay the freight. I didn't envy those two—I hated 'em! I doubt if they got a grizzly. If they did, that poor guide sure earned his money.)

There are some additional considerations you will have to make before taking off to the bush to bust a bear. You must appraise your physical abilities. Committing yourself to an arduous wilderness hunt when you are not physically capable of spending long hours on steep mountain sides at high elevations can be sheer torture.

If you are over forty, I suggest you get a complete physical check up. While you are there, tell your doctor about your plans and ask him to suggest an exercise program. Even if you are in good physical shape, you are probably not in good physical condition. Join an exercise club and work out on a regular basis. Regular, vigorous exercise will not only improve your cardiopulmonary and cardiovascular system, but you will also trim off a lot of baby fat. Ten pounds of excess Crisco can take a terrible toll when you are chasing a guide who is half mountain goat up a mountain with its top stuck up in the clouds. It will take a year or so to set up your trip, so start your conditioning program at the same time you start scanning magazines for names of guides.

If you will be traveling to a base camp, or hunting from horseback, spend some time at the local rent-a-horse establishment. I once had a friend who worked for an eastern hunting lodge. He spent a big portion of every working day outdoors walking in the woods. Once we went elk hunting in Colorado and spent our first day on horseback.

Well, actually he spent the first half day on horseback. His butt got to hurting him so bad that, after just two or three hours, he unloaded and started walking. He didn't sit or lie on his back for the rest of the hunt; he was even too sore to walk. If you have never been saddle sore, the feeling is something like the way you would feel if you sat on a fire hydrant for three or four hours straight. After about the third day, you feel much better—sort of like sitting and soaking in rubbing alcohol!

Outdoor writers often emphasize the importance of getting into condition by jogging prior to going on a hunt in a mountainous area. That is good advice. But I rarely see much reference to getting your butt in shape for spending days in the saddle. I have seen hunters literally crippled (not permanently) for days because they had not toughened up their tails enough to sit on a horse for several hours a day.

I recommend going into a vigorous riding program months before taking your trip. Just as with any other conditioning program, start off early with light workouts and build up slowly to more saddle time. An hour is sufficient a few times a week to get started. Just before leaving on your trip, you should have progressed to being able to spend at least half a day in the saddle with no ill effects.

Another advantage of an extensive riding program is that you will learn to ride a horse. Some stables offer riding instructions—take them. A pack trip in the Rockies is not the place to learn!

Once, another buddy of mine went on a hunt with a brand-new pair of boots. He had blisters the size of pigeon eggs by lunch time. If you suspect your faithful old boots won't be up to an extended bear hunting expedition, get a new pair several months in advance and wear them around the house, to the store, or even to work if the dress code allows it. The remote back country is not the place to break in new footwear.

As soon as you have selected a guide, ask for his recommendations on rifles, calibers, and sights. His advice on the right firearm is the best you can obtain because he alone knows the terrain you will be hunting in, how you will be hunting, and at what distances you will be shooting.

Once you have obtained your chosen firearm, shoot it—then shoot it some more. Shoot it from a bench rest at known distances to sight it in. Then shoot it at various distances so you will know where it shoots at 50 yards, 100 yards, 200 yards, and on out to the maximum distance you are capable of placing your shots accurately. If you have access to a metallic silhouette range, it wouldn't be a bad idea to spend some time there. Shooting a few rounds at silhouettes won't make you into an expert marksman, but it will acquaint you with the realities of long range shooting and dispel any myths you may have about hitting a grizzly right between the eyes at a distance of four football fields.

You should spend as much time as possible shooting your rifle from sitting, kneeling, and resting positions. The prone (lying down) position is very steady and conducive to accurate bullet placement, but rarely is it practical in hunting situations. The least desirable shooting position of all is standing upright on your legs (like John Wayne in the movies) and blasting away. If you have a choice when offered a shot, use one of the more stable positions rather than the standing offhand position.

The very best exercise for walking in mountainous country is walking up and down steep hills. If you don't have steep hills, use the steps of the local football stadium. Walk the stadium steps sideways, which is how most people traverse the side of a hill. It is important that you do some of your uphill walking on sloping ground rather than just on steps as you won't find many steps cut into the mountain sides in bear country. Walking on a sloping surface stretches muscles and tendons that are not subjected to stress when climbing steps.

As the time for your departure draws near, request a list of what you should bring with you from your guide. Most guides are glad to do this since having what you need and not having what you don't need will make his job easier.

5

Accessories and Equipment

"Necessities for bear hunting" would have probably been a more accurate title for this chapter. There are many types of equipment which increase your chances of success and make the job of getting head, hide, and meat out of the woods much easier when you do score. The best advice for selecting hunting accessories when using a guide is to ask him for a list of things to bring. It won't be necessary to ask the guide who is a real pro for a list. The real pro will enclose a list, including everything from underwear to raingear.

I probably take along a bunch of junk that I don't need, but on some occasions my junk comes in mighty handy. Anytime and every-time I go into the bush, I carry waterproof matches, a compass, and a sturdy knife, all are attached on a nylon cord to my belt and tucked into my pants pocket, not in a vest or jacket pocket that may be left back in camp. It is hard for someone who is even as absent minded as I am to forget his pants! These are survival items, not just accessories.

A small day pack is mighty handy for carrying some additional gear such as a drag rope. The hunter who kills his first bear is often in for a big surprise. There are no convenient handles on a bear like the antlers on a deer, so you don't have anyplace to grab them for the purpose of moving them.

I once came upon a first-time successful bear hunter in the mountains near my home. He was on the verge of total exhaustion. The bear he was attempting to drag, carry, slide, and otherwise move off the mountain had just about worn him out. I suggested we use his belt like a dog collar so we could drag the bear to a nearby road I knew about. We were hunting on a management area which required the bear carcass be brought out ungutted and intact.

I include a drag rope in my daypack for occasions such as this when I have to move a bear. Baker Manufacturing Company makes one that has a wide nylon shoulder strap, which makes the chore a little easier. A length of nylon rope will suffice if you tie it to a short, sturdy limb to use as a handle.

Binoculars are a necessity, even in the dense cover of the eastern bear habitat. They are invaluable for a close inspection of a bear's pelt to determine if it is in good condition and free of any rubbed spots. This is particularly important on late spring and early fall hunts when the pelts are not prime. Binoculars are also worth their weight in those situations when you see a suspicious object at a great distance that may or may not be a bear. A good pair of binoculars will often eliminate any unnecessary, time-consuming stalks where you discover that the "bear" you have been sneaking up on was just a rotten log. For all practical purposes, 7 × 35 power binoculars will be the best single choice for most types of bear hunting. It is difficult for most folks to hand-hold a set more powerful than this.

A bear is a challenge to get out of the woods, especially if you have never had the experience before. Not only do they lack antlers, but you can't drag them by the legs because their wrists are so wide you can't reach around them with your fingers to get a good grip. In most cases, recruit assistance if at all possible.

We were hauling a cinnamon bear out of the Rockies once and we had about a mile and a half to the road. The bear weighed about three hundred pounds. We had five guys in the party to handle the chore. One fellow carried a Coleman lantern and led the way. The rest of us carried the bear out. How did we grab hold? Gary Ginther showed me one of the neatest tricks I have ever seen. We rolled the bear onto his stomach and then one of us grabbed him at the elbows and at each knee and we lifted him up (after he had been gutted, of course). If you lay a bear on his back and try to pick him up by his legs, he will bend into a "U" shape, and you won't even be able to get him off the ground. If you lay him on his stomach and have four guys each lift at the elbows and knees, that bear will come up off the ground like he is lying face down on a stretcher. His legs will not bend back past a horizontal position, and his back will bend straight and no further.

In some situations a spotting scope on a tripod is mighty handy. Two I can think of right offhand are hunting grizzlies in the spring and hunting black bears in berries in northern Canada in the fall. In the spring, when grizzlies first come out of their dens, they frequently feed on grass. They will graze just like a big old silver-tipped cow. The first places that show green grass in the Rockies in the spring time are what is referred to as slides. During the winter, snow slides or avalanches will scour large areas of mountain sides bare of trees and rocks, leaving loose, bare soil. These bare spots or slides warm up real quick in the spring and sprout the tender young grass that the grizzlies feed on.

Experienced hunters will ease up onto a ridge overlooking several of these slides and set up a spotting scope which is used to thoroughly glass each slide for a feeding bear. Sometimes several bears may be observed at once with this technique. In this happy situation, a spotting scope is the only reliable way to determine which bear is the best trophy and most desirable to hunt.

In late summer and early fall, black bears in northeastern Canada feed heavily on blueberries. Some of these patches are immense, and the only way to search them visually is from some promontory with a good high-powered spotting scope. The bigger the berry patch, the better your chances of seeing a bear.

A rifle scope sight is invaluable in many types of bear hunting. Hunting bears in the Rockies, in interior Alaska and the berry patches of northern Canada often require shots longer than point-blank range. I also prefer a scope-sighted rifle for watching a bait. It affords very precise shot placement at either end of the day when my middle-aged eyes have trouble seeing a set of open sights against a coal black bear pelt.

I prefer a low-power variable scope, such as a 1 to 5X, for hunting over a bait and a 3 to 9X for work in more open country. All the scopes on bear rifles should have see-through scope mounts. I prefer these mounts just in case I have to do some impromptu close-range work. A scope is worse than useless at a range of a few steps, and that is when a bear is really dangerous because your field of vision through the scope will be blurred or entirely filled with what appears to be fields of black wheat. All you will be able to see is bear hair, with no way of determining if that hair is over his chest or his butt.

A good sturdy knife is a necessity for gutting and stripping the upholstery of any bruin you are lucky enough to collect. I have field-dressed bears with pocket knives, a custom Randall knife worth several hundred dollars, a Green River mountain man knife I made from a kit, and other assorted cutlery. Field dressing a black bear is not much different than gutting a big whitetail deer. In both cases I prefer to have a knife that is sturdy enough to go through the pelvic arch (pelvic bone). Severing the pelvic arch greatly facilitates the cooling of the hindquarters of an animal that cannot be cut up into quarters immediately. A small whetstone or one of the handy broadhead sharpeners used by bowhunters can be used to touch up a knife blade when gutting, quartering, and skinning a big bear.

Insect repellant is necessary on most bear hunts. On spring bear hunts in the north country, bug dope is more important than your rifle. I know of two separate hunting trips to Ontario in late May that were cancelled on the second day because the hunters were being eaten alive by blackflies while they sat over a bear bait. Those blackflies will eat you up quicker than any bear you ever saw!

On one of my spring hunts to Ontario, I shot a bear about two hours before dark. I gutted him and moved him near a road where I was to meet my partner after dark. Gutting that bear and getting him to the meeting place was hot, thirsty work. I propped the carcass open with some sticks to cool and went in search of some cool water. I found a small spring in a deep ravine nearby, and after quenching my thirst I washed the blood off my hands and forearms. I then reapplied insect repellant to my hands and forearms but missed a narrow strip on the under side of my right forearm.

I returned to the spot where I had left my bear and stretched out for a nap to wait for the arrival of my buddy. That night back in camp, the spot I had missed began to itch. The more I scratched, the more I itched. By the next morning, my arm was covered with hundreds of tiny bumps which later had white, festered cores in them. It was several weeks before the itching stopped and the sores healed. I can believe the stories I have heard about blackflies driving people insane.

There are several good blackfly repellants: Deep Woods Off, 6-12, and Cutters. Just recently a new product called Ben's 100 has come out, and I have heard some good things about it. I have a trip scheduled for the north country this year, and I plan to give it a field test.

I cannot overemphasize the importance of taking an abundant supply of insect repellant to the north country in the spring. After you have what you think is an ample supply, double it! Some people prefer head nets and many hunters do use them. I would rather douse myself liberally with repellant since I am bothered by looking through the mesh of a head net.

Durable rain gear and hip boots are essential if your hunt will take you to southeastern or coastal Alaska. They are also valuable items just about anywhere you hunt bears, especially on a spring hunt when weather is apt to be wet and unpredictable. If I have booked a ten-day hunt and it rains for ten days straight, then I will hunt for ten days in the rain. I don't think any hunter will want to sit out even one day's hunting nor hunt while soaked to the skin.

6

Guns, Loads, and Sights

On more than one occasion I have read an article in which some outdoor scribe recommends, "any rifle used for whitetail deer" as "adequate for black bear." If you select a bear rifle on the sole basis that it is a dandy whitetail choice, you are asking for trouble. There are several very good reasons why the "ideal" whitetail rifle is not a good choice for black bears.

It is possible to kill a black bear with a .22 rimfire and many people have. It is possible to kill a bear with a sharp teaspoon, but I don't recommend that, either! Unlike a wounded whitetail, a wounded bear can do a hunter serious damage; a dying but aroused bear can still live long enough to injure or kill his opponent. A bear must be shot with a rifle powerful enough to break him down and anchor him. Once a bear gets his adrenaline up, you have to stop him, and that takes a firearm with enough wallop to shoot through massive bone structure.

Most blacks will quickly flee when shot, but some will press a

If all shots were taken at this range and angle, and all bears were the size of this small black, then a deer rifle would be adequate for bear. But neither situation is the norm. (Photo courtesy of the Government of Saskatchewan)

charge. I have only had one black bear fail to try to escape when I shot him. I hit him in the left shoulder, and the bullet stopped inside the body cavity just in front of his right hip. The bullet missed the shoulder bone but destroyed the left lung and caused massive bleeding. It was about twenty-five minutes before I was able to place the second shot that broke his back and finished him. But remember: A wounded bear only needs a few seconds to give you a slap or a chomp, and if one does, you will not enjoy it!

When a wounded bear runs off, a hunter following the blood trail could be in a lot of trouble when the bear realizes he cannot get away due to his injury. A wounded bear that has been tracked to a hiding place is more apt to attack than one that is first startled by a gunshot.

Another fallacy in the theory that any old whitetail rifle is good for black bears is the vast difference in the physical structure of the two animals. A deer is built for speed, with relatively light weight and fragile bone structure. A bear is powerfully built for rolling over logs, digging, climbing, and doing battle with other bears over mating and territorial rights. They are as different in body mass and anatomical design as a marathon runner and a sumo wrestler.

If conditions permit, and you have the time and correct angle to place something like a .100-caliber bullet out of a .243 or 6mm Remington right between a bear's ribs into his lungs, he will probably drop in his tracks. Therefore, under ideal conditions, I would say any .25-caliber bullet with enough punch to drop a whitetail would be adequate. But when you deal with reality and accept the fact that the broadside standing shot that is so often depicted and discussed in sporting journals rarely presents itself in the wild, then you will put aside high-velocity pill shooters and select a firearm that propels a bullet with sufficient mass to survive a collision with a bear's superstructure.

A marginal bear rifle/cartridge combination won't do the job, even if you place your shot behind the shoulder, because if you do get in trouble with a bear that would rather fight than switch locations, that bear is not going to charge you sideways. He will charge you head on with a lot of big muscle and massive bones between you and that deadly lung shot that the devotees of the marginal bear rifle expound on so frequently.

It is best to choose a rifle-cartridge combination that can reach a vital area with enough punch to do maximum damage from a raking shot that must pass through masses of non-vital flesh or bones. I do not mean to imply that with a powerful rifle you can shoot a bear anywhere and anchor him. A shot that goes into one side of a bear's abdomen and comes out the other side results in nothing more than a gut-shot bear doomed to extensive suffering (and very likely to inflict the same on the hunter), no matter how powerful the rifle. However, a rifle with enough punch can enter a bear's abdomen behind the last rib, pass through the vital areas of the chest, and break the shoulder on the opposite side—if the angle of the shot is available to the hunter.

I know four Rocky Mountain big game guides who carry an 1895 Marlin lever action chambered for the venerable .45-70 Government. (This is a modern rifle, even though the model number sounds antique.) The first time I ran across a guide with a .45-70 in his saddle boot, I asked him why he didn't have one of the modern magnums. He answered that a magnum is fine for long range shots, but a bear is not dangerous at a range of two football fields. A bear is dangerous when

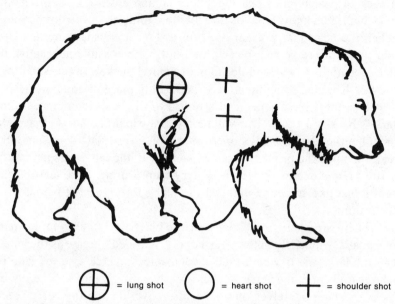

= lung shot   = heart shot   = shoulder shot

A bear rifle shot has to pack enough punch to pierce the animal's forequarters, break both of its shoulders (possibly entering the heart or lungs in the process) so it will be anchored. Then, and only then, can the bear be finished off.

you get "close enough to dance with him." At those ranges a quick pointing, fast shooting lever gun is hard to beat, he said.

I thought he was wrong in his selection of a rifle for following up wounded blacks until I ran across three other guides, who told me the same story. I am a convert. Now when I go on a bear hunt I take two rifles. One is an 8mm Remington Magnum Model 700 BDL, and the other is an 1895 Marlin chambered for the .45-70 Government. I shoot handloads in the .45-70 since factory ammo is loaded to very low pressures to avoid blowing up the old trap door Springfields that are still frequently shot. My best .45-70 bear load comes right out of the *Hornady Handbook* and consists of 47.1 grains of IMR 4198 behind a 350-grain round nose bullet (#4502). **This is a maximum load. Use with caution!**

On several occasions when I have been chasing bears with hounds, I have selected the big-bore 94 chambered for the .375 Winchester. The big-bore 94 totes nice, and if you have ever tried to keep up with a pack of bear hounds chasing a bear up and down the southern Appalachians you know that you do a lot more toting than you do shooting. When the bear does present itself for a shot, it is usually up in a tree and you can pretty well place your shot. One possible alternative to this scenario is a bear-and-dog fight in a laurel thicket. In this situation, the fast-handling little big-bore 94 is a handy piece of equipment.

This fall I have scheduled a return to the bear country near Ontario's Kirkland Lake. This will be my first trip in the fall. Our agenda includes the last few days of trout season, some partridge shooting, and of course the primary objective—bear. In the fall, bears get pretty serious about decimating the blueberry crop. During berry season bear scat looks like someone dumped the filling for blueberry pie all over the ground.

There are some tremendously large blueberry patches in this part of Canada, especially in the clear-cut or "scarified" areas, as the locals call the large tracts where timber companies have cleared the land of all trees. We hunt the berry patches in early morning and late afternoons by positioning ourselves on an elevation overlooking the berry patch from the downwind side. A good pair of binoculars or a spotting scope is mighty handy. It is also a good idea to select a lookout point that doesn't skylight you against the horizon.

This type of bear hunting often presents some long range shots. What is a long range shot? It depends on your rifle, your cartridge, your sights, and your ability to shoot. To get a grasp of the realities of long range shooting, haul yourself off to a rifle range that offers silhouette shooting. When you can stand upright on your legs and knock over that ram with the iron pants at 400 meters with regularity, then you can justify taking such a shot in the field on live game.

It is important to know your limitations as a marksman, your rifle's capability for placing a shot precisely where you aim it, and your cartridge's ability to do lethal damage at extended range. The only way you can determine these facts is to spend a lot of time shooting your rifle at long range and studying the ballistics of your particular firearm.

The real secret to long range shooting is practice and cheating. By cheating, I mean using a rest whenever possible. A rifle that is propped on a rock or log with a hat or jacket under the fore end of the rifle will do wonders for your shooting ability. Never place the rifle barrel on anything solid when shooting from a rest as this will cause the rifle to shoot high. Rest the rifle on the fore end of the stock, preferably with some sort of cushion between the stock and the rest. Practice long range shooting from prone, sitting, kneeling and standing positions. However, it is very difficult to place long range shots from a standing position accurately. (Forget how many times you saw John Wayne in the movies knock over outlaws two counties away while shooting a .30-30 with open sights from a standing position.)

Bear rifles are often compromise choices. A rifle that is adequate for a mule deer or a 150-pound black bear would be a doubtful choice for a 400-pound black or a 600-pound grizzly. If you select a rifle capable of dumping a grizzly in his tracks, then you might consider yourself overgunned for a small black bear. Believe me—overdoing it is the lesser of the two evils. It is much better to be overgunned on smaller game than encounter a big dose of adrenaline-filled bear and not have a firearm with enough punch to bring the encounter to a favorable conclusion. When hunting several types of game, select a firearm for the biggest and toughest species you expect to encounter.

I would not presume to prophesy on the proper bear rifle any more than I would pontificate on selecting a spouse, automobile, or pair of shoes for hunting. A rifle-cartridge combo is a personal choice that must be made by each individual hunter. If you are going on a guided hunt, ask your guide about how you will be hunting, ranges at which you can expect to make shots, and his suggestions on firearms and calibers. Your guide has probably witnessed more bear kills than any other single person you will ever hunt with, so take advantage of his experience.

SUGGESTED RIFLES AND LOADS FOR BLACK BEARS

As I stated previously, I consider the .243 Winchester and 6mm Remington to be marginal black bear rifles, not because they lack the foot-pounds of energy required to kill a bear under the right conditions, but simply because I want a bullet that has more mass and is more durable than the high-velocity, 100-grain pill these two calibers propel. I am well aware that these two calibers are adequate for black bears when you look at ballistic tables. I know many hunters have dropped blacks in their tracks with these two rounds; you may have even accomplished this feat yourself. All I am saying is that if I had some other choices, I would not select either of these two as my primary choice for a black bear rifle.

A bear of these proportions will require more "medicine" than a small, lightweight bullet can provide. (Photo courtesy of the Government of Quebec)

If you shoot a healthy bear in the fall, he will have a rather substantial layer of fat several inches thick under his hide. This layer of fat has an annoying capability of plugging up bullet holes, making the chore of tracking a wounded bear extremely difficult. This is one of the reasons I prefer a big-bore bullet that has the energy to pass all the way through a bear. This gives you two wounds leaving blood signs which (even someone with my poor mathematical skills can figure out) will double your tracking odds.

Every month or so one of the gun magazines will have an article discussing that old question, "Which load is best? The one that stays inside the animal and expends all its energy, or the one that exits the other side, making a longer wound channel and creating two exit wounds?" I don't think there is any one simple correct answer to that question. (Apparently the folks who write for the gun mags don't think so either because the controversy sure gets a lot of attention.)

A bear has a thick, woolly coat when he is right out of his den during the spring hunt and again during the fall season when he is preparing to go back into the den for the winter. This thick, woolly coat can act like a sponge and soak up considerable amounts of blood from a wound. This fact supports my argument for big-bore bullets.

I do not mean to imply from these arguments that the hunter should take any shot which presents itself, assuming that he can track and finish any bear he wounds. I'm emphatic that you should not take any shot that does not have a very high percentage of dropping that bear right where he stands. There are times when sighting errors or other factors prevent an instant kill, and a tracking job then becomes necessary. This is the contingency I am allowing for when I suggest you select a shooting iron that is a little on the heavy side rather than an alternative that may be marginal on the other end of the scale.

Up until now I have focused primarily upon calibers and bullets. Selecting an action is also a prime consideration. If you have a decided preference for bolt, autoloading, slide, or lever action, and are used to using that rifle, then that is a good choice to consider first. Each action design has specific advantages. The bolt action is inherently the most accurate. But have you ever seen a serious competitive target shooter

A successful hunter shown with an old Winchester Model 94, chambered for the .30-30. The Winchester is still popular with many sportsmen who hunt bears with dogs; however, there are better gun choices for the modern hunter. (Photo courtesy of Florida Game and Freshwater Fish Commission)

using a slide, autoloading, or lever action? Did you ever see a serious varmint shooter use one of these? Nope. Me neither. I'll tell you something else you won't see: someone follow a wounded bear into the bush toting a seventeen-pound bench rest rifle with a 10-power Unertal scope, unless he wants to club the bruin to death! Again, I emphasize the importance of asking your guide for suggestions, since he knows more precisely the type of terrain, ranges, and other conditions where the shooting will be done.

If you have patiently read up to this point in this chapter in search of my suggestion for the "absolute, ideal, prime black bear rifle," then search no more—because I don't believe any such varmint exists. I don't know of one, I suspect there never has been one, and there probably never will be one because bears are hunted under such a wide variety of conditions.

I am prepared to list a number of calibers and actions for certain types of bear hunting to assist you in making your own choice.

HUNTING WITH DOGS

Most of this shooting will be at either a treed animal or one that is in a knock-down, drag-out scrap with the dogs. Chasing dogs is very strenuous, so I suggest a short, light, easy to carry rifle.

Actions: Lever, slide, autoloading

Calibers: .30-30 Winchester, 170-grain; .35 Remington, 200-grain; .300 Savage, 180-grain; .308 Winchester, 180-grain; .30-06, 180-grain; .32 Winchester Special, 170-grain; .348 Winchester, 200-grain; .358 Winchester, 250-grain; .375 Winchester, 250-grain; .44 Remington Magnum, 265-grain; .444 Marlin, 265-grain; .45-70 Government, 405-grain.

HUNTING BEARS OVER BAIT

Watching a bait will present the hunter with a wide variety of possible shots: a close shot at a bear unaware of your presence; a long-range shot at a bear that has winded you, or for some other reason is suspicious and refuses to approach any closer; or a bear that has suddenly become aware of your presence at the bait and bolts into high gear. Many shots are taken right at dusk in thickly wooded areas, where the light gathering properties of a good high quality scope will allow the precise shot placement that is difficult with open sights in poor light. Although I will list several actions and calibers, my preference for this type of bear hunting under most conditions is bolt action rifle of at least .30-06 caliber with a low power variable scope such as a 1X to 4X.

Rifle actions: Bolt, lever, slide, or autoloader

Calibers: .270 Winchester, 150-grain; .270 Weatherby Magnum, 150-grain; 7mm-08 Remington, 175-grain; 7 × 57, 140 or 175 grain; .284 Winchester, 150-grain; .280 Remington or 7mm Express, 175-grain; 7mm Remington Magnum, 175-grain; .300 Savage, 180-grain; .308 Winchester, 180-grain; .30-06, 180-grain; .300 Winchester Magnum, 180-grain; 8mm Remington Magnum, 185-grain

Some of the cartridges in the preceding list may seem excessive for a 150-pound black bear. I would agree they are. I also contend they are not excessive for a 400-pound-plus trophy-class black bear. I would rather be prepared for a "bragging size" bear with a gun that will anchor him on the spot, than be caught with a pea shooter which was only marginally adequate.

RIFLES FOR STALKING BEARS IN OPEN COUNTRY

When hunting bears over berry patches or other open country, where shots will be taken at relatively longer ranges than when hunting with dogs or over bait, your rifle and load should be chosen with this in mind.

Rifle action: Bolt

Calibers: .270 Winchester, 150-grain; .270 Weatherby Magnum, 150-grain; .280 Remington or 7mm Express, 150-grain; 7mm Remington Magnum, 175-grain; 7mm Weatherby Magnum, 175-grain; .30-06, 180-grain; .300 Winchester Magnum, 180-grain; .300 Weatherby Magnum, 180-grain; 8mm Remington Magnum.

RIFLES AND LOADS FOR GRIZZLY, BROWN, AND POLAR BEAR

I'll give you the bottom line first: the best rifle for grizzly, brown, or polar bear is the most powerful one you can shoot accurately. I consider the .30-06 to be the absolute minimum rifle for the big bears.

The author with a bear he killed with one of his favorite bear rifles—a Remington 700 BDL chambered for the 8mm Remington Magnum.

I would not personally use a .30-06 unless I was in trouble with a bear and had nothing more powerful to use. I also do not recommend using cartridges without belted cases.

Rifle actions: Bolt action and Browning autoloader

Calibers: 7mm Remington Magnum, 175-grain; 300 Winchester Magnum, 220-grain; 300 Weatherby, 220-grain; 8mm Remington Magnum, 220-grain; 338 Winchester Magnum, 250-grain; 340 Weatherby Magnum, 250-grain; 375 H&H Magnum, 300-grain; 378 Weatherby, 300-grain; 458 Winchester Magnum, 350-grain.

When selecting a bullet for one of the big bears, you must temper your choice based upon the type of terrain. If you were hunting brown bears in alder thickets along an Alaskan salmon stream, it would be desirable to have the largest bullet available in the caliber you were shooting. If

When a grizzly like this one comes your way, the best rifle to break him is the most powerful one that you can shoot accurately. (Photo by R.J. Hayes)

you were hunting browns on the beach as they were eating sedge grass in the spring, you might want to use a lighter bullet to get the flatter trajectory for this longer range shooting.

The bottom line bears repeating: the best rifle for grizzly, brown, and polar bear is the most powerful rifle you can shoot accurately.

SIGHTS

Open sights are probably the best choice for hunting bears behind dogs because the traveling is rough, and shots are taken anywhere from close range to "dancing" distance. If you must have a scope for this type of bear hunting it should have no more magnification than 1X. At a distance of a few yards, bear upholstery will fill a scope entirely, and it is extremely difficult to identify exactly which portion of the bruin's anatomy you are looking at.

A scope is desirable for shooting over a bait. In most situations you will get the first shot before the bear knows you are around. A scope will allow for a more precise shot placement, especially during the last moments of dusk when the biggest percentage of bears will approach a bait. A low power variable scope is a good choice.

A scope is a necessity for shooting in open country at the longer ranges. The best scope in the world won't help you if you don't know where your rifle shoots at the longer ranges. It is rather silly for a man to spend several thousand dollars for a bear hunt and then lose a real trophy just because he can't shoot!

I am a firm believer in see-through scope mounts for bear hunting. You never know when you will encounter a bear at a distance of only a few paces, have one charge you at close range, or follow a wounded one into the bush. For social occasions such as these, a see-through scope mount is just about the best life insurance around.

HANDLOADING

Even with the extensive selection of cartridges and bullets available across the counter, the bear hunter would be wise to consider the advantages of handloading his own ammunition. Handloading your own ammo has several advantages. You can select a bullet for your particular rifle that may be better suited to your hunting techniques. The

Bears are most active at the beginning and end of each day. A scope will allow you to place shots more accurately during these low light periods. (Photo courtesy of Tennessee Wildlife Resources Agency)

lists in this chapter consist of commercially available factory-loaded ammunition. The handloader can expand on these lists considerably.

With some research and enjoyable experimentation, the handloader can work up a bullet and powder charge that will produce the optimum accuracy in a rifle.

Space restrictions prohibit the inclusion of handloading data for bear hunting cartridges. There are several excellent basic handloading manuals available, and they can be found in sporting goods emporiums which carry handloading gear. Both the Hornady and Speer reloading manuals contain handloading data on most of the bear cartridges I have discussed.

There is one more formidable firearm for dispatching bruins, especially at close range. When a bear gets within biting or clawing distance, nothing can beat a quick-pointing 12 gauge loaded with slugs or buckshot. When Glacier National Park Rangers had to go into the bush after the two grizzlies that killed and partially devoured Mary Patricia Mahoney in 1976, they knew they were confronting known maneaters. What did they choose to arm themselves with? A 12-gauge shotgun loaded with slugs.

A 12-gauge shotgun loaded with slugs or 00 buckshot would not even be on my list as a choice grizzly, brown or polar bear hunting firearm. But it would be number one on my list as a weapon to be carried by a salmon fisherman or for quick access in a camp in bear country. As a purely self defense firearm in grizzly country the slugs or 00 buckshot would be the most effective life insurance you could carry, but the range is too limited to hope it would be effective at the ranges most bears are seen in hunting situations.

7

Hunting With Handguns

Many hunters opt to add additional spice to the sport of bear hunting by decreasing their firepower to something less than one of the big-bore magnums which spew mushroom-shaped clouds upon ignition. The man who chooses to hunt bears with a bow, black powder firearm, or handgun is certainly taking on an additional challenge. He also takes on an additional obligation—an obligation to the game animal he is hunting. That obligation dictates that the hunter becomes proficient in the use of his chosen weapon. It is the hunter's duty to practice, practice, practice, and then to only shoot at an animal that is well within his effective range.

I consider only one gun to be adequate for black bear hunting—the .44 magnum. I do not recommend handguns for hunting grizzly, browns, or polar bears. I know it is legal in some states and provinces where the big bears are found, and I am also aware that sporting literature is strewn with stories of "How I Busted a Brownie With My

Big-Bore Handgun.'' But shooting one of the big bears with a handgun is a stunt that can only be pulled off by a man who is ranked somewhere above expert as a marksman, who can stalk to within spitting distance of a big bear, and then be cool enough to put a bullet into a target area that may be no larger than a man's hand. I repeat: Just putting a round through a bear's chest won't do. You have to break him down to be absolutely sure that he won't run off and die a lingering death or live long enough to jump on you.

The distance from shooter to target will be short when you hunt with a handgun. You can expect some unpredictable reactions when you cook off a .44 mag while standing within ''dancing distance'' of a bear. Bear experts agree that one of the real no-no's is surprising a bear at close quarters. And I can't think of anything that would surprise a bear or infuriate him more than shooting him from a few feet away in some portion of his anatomy that was not immediately fatal. A grizzly could have you on the ground and dead before the echoes of your first shot had died away!

You can expect some real fireworks when you shoot a bear at this close a range with a handgun. But this should never be attempted without having an experienced hunter standing by with a powerful rifle as a backup. (Photo by R.J. Hayes)

My friend, R.J. Hayes, who is an Alaskan wildlife photographer and writer, shares my philosophy concerning the use of handguns on grizzly and other big bears. I quote the knowledgeable Mr. Hayes: "You might try killing a grizzly with your handgun, but remember to save one bullet for yourself!"

I have packed my Model 629, .44 Magnum Smith & Wesson when salmon fishing in case some resident brown bear decided to execute me for trespassing on what he considered his own private stretch of angling real estate. In cases where local regulations gave me a choice between my .44 handgun and my .45-70 lever action rifle stuffed with handloads, it was the .45-70 lever action that got to go salmon fishing. I have been in a few situations in Alaska when I was fishing or photographing bears when my handgun felt mighty good riding in my shoulder holster. On one or two occasions I have even taken it out of the leather when trouble looked imminent. Fortunately, I have never had to bust a handgun primer in a big bear's face, and I hope I never have to.

For some types of black bear hunting, a handgun is a pretty good choice of artillery. If you are going to be chasing bears with dogs, then a handgun totes mighty nicely if you are traveling via foot or horseback. Most of the shots taken behind dogs are at relatively close range with the bear either treed or beating up on the dogs in a fight on the ground.

I would recommend a handgun only if you are going to be actually running with the dogs. (I should rephrase that—running *after* them would be much more accurate.) If you are waiting on stand while the dogs are running, then I would recommend a rifle of adequate caliber.

There are a few places where I would not recommend using handguns, even for chasing bears with dogs—the places where the trees look like Jack's bean stalk. Two such places I can think of are the California redwood forests and Joyce Kilmer National Forest in western North Carolina, where I've hunted bears a few times. (Joyce Kilmer wrote the famous poem, "Trees." When you see the size of the virgin poplar, pines and other huge trees, you can understand why they picked this particular piece of forest to honor Kilmer.) These trees are so high I am sure there must be several communication satellites snagged in the uppermost branches. Either location would require considerable handgun skill to place an accurate shot on a treed bear.

Do not assume that just because a bear is treed you have an easy handgun shot. Bears are prone to come out of a tree when approached by hunters. I have known bears to jump out of trees several times and take off running all over again. Always approach a bear quietly and slowly when it is treed. If several hunters run up under the tree shouting and making a lot of noise, you can bet that bear is going to bolt and be gone before you get close enough to tag him with a well-placed shot.

Whenever possible, use some sort of rest to steady your sight picture. I don't care if your physical condition parallels that of an Olympic marathoner—you are going to be trembling from exertion after chasing a pack of dogs over mountains, across streams, and through thickets. I also guarantee you that your trembling will be shifted up into spasmodic jerks when you see that bear perched up in a tree and your body gives you a big squirt of adrenaline.

None of these conditions aid in the accurate shooting of handguns. The problem is further compounded by the fact that you will be shooting almost straight up at an elusive target that will put as many limbs and as much tree trunk between you as possible. If you think shooting a black bear out of a tree with a handgun is similar to punching holes in a bull's-eye at the local gun club range, think again.

To keep movement under the tree to a minimum, select the best possible spot to shoot from before you approach the tree. One of the prime considerations to look for when selecting a spot is something to use for a rest.

Many guides who hunt with dogs carry handguns. Bear hounds are very expensive, and no dog owner wants a bear to send several thousand dollars worth of pooch to doggie heaven or maul him so severely that he has to go on canine disability.

When bears and dogs get into a melee, a handgun at close range is just about the best way to bring the festivities to a halt. The guide will usually wade right in and put a few close ones where they will do the most good. I don't recommend that you try this yourself. It takes a very aggressive dog to do close quarters combat with a bear. Once dogs get worked up, they can be almost as dangerous as a bear. Never attempt to wade into a bear-dog fight if you are not thoroughly familiar with the dogs. If you are in business, being a middle man can be very profitable. Being the middle man in a bear-hound fight can result in losing great chunks out of your anatomy.

I once had a native Alaskan tell me that he could spot a "chee-chaco" (a greenhorn or someone on his first trip to Alaska) a mile away. He always had three things: a beard, a husky dog, and a .44

magnum pistol to keep the bears out of his britches. Many resident Alaskans who work or travel in bear country keep a .44 mag handy. This is mostly a matter of convenience since it is impossible to keep a rifle handy and get much work done. Those folks who know a little something about bears and have more than just a passing knowledge of handguns realize that any handgun is not much more than a last-ditch alternative to being torn apart.

Under *no* circumstances should anyone shoot a grizzly, brown, or polar bear with a handgun unless they have someone standing by who is capable of stopping a charging bear with a big-bore high powered rifle. Your chances of dropping one of the big bears right in his tracks with one shot—or even several for that matter—are somewhere between slim and none.

My choices for black bear hunting handguns would include the model 29 or 629 .44 Magnum Smith & Wesson or the Ruger Redhawk in the same caliber. Both of these handguns are double-action revolvers made by manufacturers with well-deserved reputations for producing dependable, accurate firearms.

There are a few wildcat cartridges which approximate .44 magnum energies, but since these are cases of custom guns and handloaded ammo, they are outside the realm of the average bear hunter.

At this time a new .45-caliber magnum autoloading pistol is in the works. But since I have seen neither the cartridge nor the pistol "in the flesh" I will refrain from comment until I evaluate the piece in the future.

8

Hunting with Muzzleloaders

It was inevitable that the increase in the popularity of hunting with muzzle-loading firearms would spread into the sport of bear hunting. In fact, bears have had a significant influence upon the design of muzzle-loading firearms. When the mountain men of the early 1800s went west to seek fortunes in fur in the "shining mountains," they often encountered a rather rude, aggressive resident known as the grizzly bear, which would absorb the puny .40-caliber lead pills from their long barrel Kentucky rifles and severely injure, even kill them. Injury or death was, of course, not one of the mountain man's primary objectives in trapping.

In order to avoid this, the trappers who roamed the Far West began to discard the small-bore Kentucky rifles and take up the Hawken rifle. The Hawken had a shorter barrel, a thicker stock, and a bigger bore than the Kentucky rifle. The shorter barrel made the Hawken easier to maneuver when the trappers got involved in shoot-outs with

The mighty grizzly was too much bear to be killed quickly with the small caliber Kentucky rifles carried by the early fur trappers who ventured into the Rockies. That's why big-bore rifles like the Hawken were developed. (Photo by R.J. Hayes)

hostile Indians. These social functions often occurred while the participants were mounted. The shorter-barreled rifles were also handy when grizzlies were encountered in the close confines of a streamside thicket. The sturdier stock was also a major improvement since it made the rifle more durable on those occasions when horse, rider, and rifle took a tumble while going full speed after buffalo or away from hostile grizzlies or Indians. The heavy-duty stock also made the rifle into a sturdy club after the charge was fired.

But the major advantage in the Hawken, and the one which made it so popular, was its larger bore of .50 or more. This bigger bore had the capability of shoving a rather substantial chunk of lead right through a grizzly's boiler room, whereas the smaller bore Kentuckies that were adequate for the eastern black bear would, more often than not, do little more to a grizzly than get him all riled up and in the mood to maul the nearest mountain man.

Because of my interest in the fur trapping area of the Rockies, I chose to use a muzzleloader on a bear hunt in that country several years ago. I can say unequivocally that was the most exciting hunting experience I have ever had. Just being in those "shining mountains" and thinking that I was maybe walking over the same ground that some fur trapper had carried his Hawken in the 1880s bordered on a religious experience for me. My imagination soared as I envisioned what that country must have been like in those days.

The flavor of that trip was heightened by an encounter with a big cinnamon bear that had the disposition of a grizzly. I had heard about the legendary "half-nosed" bear that had a reputation for tracking hunters and other deviant behavior. I pooh-poohed the stories as nothing more than local fairy tales designed to add some color and personality to that part of the southern Colorado Rockies (as if that area needed any such enhancement!).

The bear had the nickname, the "half-nosed" bear because the right half of his muzzle was missing from some previous injury. The first time I saw him I was perched on the side of a mountain with a Hawken cradled in my arms. My daydreams of mountain men and the fur trade were interrupted by the sound of what seemed to be something big rolling around a log in search of grub. Since bears spend much of their time in just such endeavors, I quickly forgot my daydreams and began to visually search the mountain above me for signs of the bear. I could not see very far due to a fairly thick stand of scrub trees.

Then, at a distance of about seventy-five yards, the bear suddenly appeared in a small opening almost as if he was one of the participants in the daydreams I had been enjoying just moments before. Seeing that bear caused such a surge of adrenaline that my respiration and pulse sounded like the engine room of the *African Queen* or the New York Philharmonic playing the "Anvil Chorus"!

Since the bear was walking almost directly toward me at a slight angle to my left, he had me pinned. I couldn't move to raise my rifle without him seeing the motion. Then his route took him behind a small but thick stand of spruce trees about five feet tall. While he was behind that thick cover, I used the opportunity to raise my rifle and place a percussion cap on the nipple. (I keep my muzzleloader cocked when I am sitting on a stand. When I get ready to shoot, I place a cap on the nipple. Putting on a cap doesn't make any noise, whereas the click-click-click of pulling a hammer to full cock could spook a bear that has come in close to a bait.)

I waited for the bear to continue in my direction and step out from behind the trees. I waited. I waited. And I waited. He still didn't show.

I have had some pretty exciting times in a life that has included riding bulls in rodeos, playing college football, setting a college track record, and scuba diving, but I felt that waiting for that bear to come out from behind those trees was the biggest thrill I had ever gotten.

The tension and excitement of waiting for the bear to appear only held that record for just a few brief moments. After about three lifetimes—probably only about two minutes in reality—the bear stepped out right where I expected him to. Then he did something I hadn't expected him to do—he looked right at me. I was in full camouflage, sitting absolutely motionless and downwind. I don't know to this day how that bear knew I was there.

Now it was decision time. I was looking at the bear through my sights which I had on his left shoulder. I couldn't see his shoulder as clearly as I would have liked since it was partially obscured by one of the small trees, but I knew the flimsy branches of that tree would not deter the 390-grain, .50-caliber Maxiball from its appointed rounds. I pulled the rear trigger on my set triggers and then touched the front one. Ignition!

The sight picture looked perfect when I cooked off that 100 grains of black powder. The resulting smoke cloud that came out the muzzle behind the bullet was so large and dense it completely obscured the bear from my sight. Then there was this god-awful roar, more of rage than pain. Next I was aware of the bear running full bore off to my left at about a forty-five degree angle. I could not believe what my eyes were seeing. I was convinced I had hit that bear right through the shoulder with nearly 400 grains of pure lead, and he didn't even go down! He didn't even stagger! He just took off like a drag racer. My gut twisted into a knot as I considered the possibility that I had missed. The confidence I had in the accuracy of my shot would ebb and flow. I began to rationalize that I had made a bad shot under the stress and excitement of seeing the bear. Then I would do a 180-degree turn and convince myself that I had indeed hit him good and he was a dead bear, but he just didn't know it.

He ran about fifty yards and turned up into some scrub brush where I could no longer see him, but I sure could hear him. He roared and busted brush and slapped saplings so hard I could see the limbs shake. It sounded like he was busting up a whole winter's supply of fire wood. I was reloading as best I could with hands that seemed to do more shaking than anything else.

   Just about the time I got reloaded, the noise stopped just as suddenly as if someone had unplugged a TV set. He's dead, I thought. I
thought wrong. After a few more moments of silence, he cranked up
the sound effects and again proceeded to rearrange the landscape. I
still couldn't see him, even though he was staying in the same area
about fifty yards away from me. He just ran back and forth and round
and round. I could see the scrub trees shaking, but I couldn't see him.
Then it got suddenly quiet again, then after a minute or so he would
erupt into a rage. This routine kept being repeated over and over for
about fifteen minutes.

   It was getting to be decision time again. I was perched in a platform
about ten feet off the ground so I could see over the underbrush. I
could not see the bear from where I was. It was about forty minutes
till dark, and I was about a mile and a half from where I was to meet
my guide in about ninety minutes. I had to descend a very steep slope
to get off the mountain. If I had a choice, the smart thing to have done
would have been to wait until daylight before following the bear. He
would probably be dead by then, and the light would also have been
better for shooting. As it was, I had two choices: I could try to negotiate
the steep slope in the dark with a flashlight in one hand, a single shot
muzzle-loading rifle in my other hand, and a wounded bear somewhere
behind me in the dark. My other choice allowed me to go into the
brush after the bear while I would still have plenty of light to shoot
and have him in front of me. At that moment, the latter sounded much
better to me, so that was what I decided to do.

   I had a small day pack with me containing a poncho, down jacket,
and some other gear. I dropped the pack to the ground first. Up until
that pack hit the ground, the only sounds the bear had made were high-
volume roars of rage that just about shook the leaves on the trees.
When that pack hit the ground, all I heard was a deep throaty roar that
was more of a growl than anything else. That was the last sound he
made.

   I removed the cap from the nipple of my rifle and lowered it to
the ground since I couldn't climb down out of the tree and hold onto
the rifle. It was a good feeling to get my feet on the ground and that
cap back on the nipple.

   I moved in the direction of the last low growl. I wasn't breaking
any speed records. I would take a very small baby step, search thoroughly, and take another tiny step. I worked my way thusly until I got

into the area where I had last heard the bear. At this stage of the game, I was trying desperately to convince myself that I would find the bear dead.

Then I saw him. I could only see the top of his head. Light was fading fast now, and I could not see his eyes. I stood there staring until my eyes watered trying to determine if he was dead or not. I was hesitant about shooting him in the head since I had my heart set on a head mount for my den wall.

Then my smarter self took command. I considered the fact that I was miles away from help, I was shooting a single shot rifle, and I had no backup if I didn't finish the job with one shot. I made my decision. As I raised the rifle to shoot him in the head, he rose up out of the bush he was in. He looked awesome! All the hair on the back of his neck was sticking straight up. His ears were laid down tight against his head. His lips were curled back. His right paw was stuck out to his side, and it looked as big as a softball glove. Then I noticed that half of his muzzle was gone, and I thought, "I didn't hit this bear in the shoulder. I haven't killed him, I just shot the end of his nose off!"

The entire preceding paragraph happened in about two heart beats.

I didn't even look at the sights on my rifle. I just pointed at the center of his chest and squeezed one off. (Precise aiming was not really necessary since a later measurement revealed the bear was only twelve long paces away when he decided to come up out of the brush and bring the fight to me.)

Just as it had on my first shot, this shot also produced a dense cloud of white smoke which completely obscured the bear. I couldn't see him but I could hear him busting brush. Then and there "the old kid" executed a strategic withdrawal (i.e., ran like hell) to try and buy some time to get another shot in.

I took off running as fast as I could and gradually increased my speed. (My college track coach would have been proud of me!) After I went about thirty yards, I didn't hear the bear any more, so I stopped and looked back. I didn't see him anywhere.

I stood right there and finished loading my rifle. It was really getting dark by now and I really wanted to get this dance over with. I eased back up the game trail in the direction where I had fired the second shot into the bear's chest. I was doing more looking than a tree full of owls.

I was able to make out a large, dark hulk setting under a large white pine that looked like an oversized oil drum. As I stared at it, I detected a switch. It was the bear's paw. He was lying on his side. I eased to the uphill side of him and kept my rifle pointing at his head. As I got closer I could see his eye was open, so I eased the muzzle of my Hawken right up to his eye and touched it. He didn't blink. He was graveyard dead.

My attention was drawn to his mangled face, and I was still amazed that I could have missed his shoulder by so much. A closer look revealed that the wound on his face had healed. Then it finally dawned on me—I had just killed the legendary "half-nosed bear" that we had heard about upon our arrival.

Both of my shots had hit where I thought they had. My first one had gone through the shoulder and, without breaking bone, had punctured the left lung, passed through the abdominal cavity, and lodged in the right rear thigh. The second shot had hit him about two inches

The author and the famous "half-nosed bear" that he killed near Salida, Colorado with a muzzle-loading rifle.

to the right of the center of his chest and exited between his shoulder blades without hitting the spine.

It was a good thing I scrammed after that second shot because he died about five steps past where I was standing when I fired. I don't know if he had enough juice left at that stage to hurt me, but I would have probably hurt myself trying to get away from him if he had started coming towards me!

At the end of the week we went to the Lamplighter Bar in Salida, Colorado to celebrate our good luck—all three hunters in our party got bears—and the demise of the "half-nosed bear." Many local hunters came to our table that night and bought a round of Coors to hear the story. (It was later published in the March 1983 issue of *Field & Stream.*) I can say that, up to now, shooting that bear with a muzzleloader was undoubtedly the most exciting experience I have ever had.

I have about a dozen muzzle-loading rifles and two muzzle-loading shotguns and do about 80 percent of all my hunting with them. Last year I hunted everything from doves to bear with these front end stuffers.

The black powder hunter has several choices when selecting a bullet for bear hunting. He may consider the round patched ball, the minnie ball, the Maxiball or the Real bullet. The minnie ball and the Maxiball are not balls at all but conical.

For black bears, I prefer at least a .50 caliber and I like to shoot a conical bullet such as the Maxiball or one of the Lee Precision Real bullets. Richard Lee sent me some of his aluminum molds last year for his Real bullets, and I have had excellent results in every one of my rifles.

My good friend Sam Fadala and I get into a conversation on our favorite subject, black powder hunting, every time we get together. Sam has written several excellent books on black powder firearms and hunting. I urge you to read all three: *The Complete Black Powder Handbook, The Black Powder Handgun,* and *The Black Powder Loading Manual.* Sam is one of the best black powder writers around, if not the best. But we do have one difference of opinion when it comes to shooting bears. Sam is an advocate of the big-bore round ball and lubricated patch. I prefer the conicals such as a Maxiball or Real. I do not disagree with Sam's position that a round ball will penetrate a bear from side to side. I am also aware that Sam has shot a round ball into the west side of a bull buffalo and it had come out the east side. My only contention is that the extra mass and momentum of a conical ball will do anything a round ball will do to a bear's plumbing and super-structure and do it better.

For those bears bigger than blacks, select a soot belcher of at least .54 caliber. I also feel obligated to suggest that if you plan to hunt the big bears with a muzzleloader, it would be wise to have someone back you up with a high-powered centerfire rifle. Your backup man should be experienced enough to put his shots where they will do the most good!

More than one bear has been lost when the black powder hunter thumbed the hammer back on his rifle. The clicking of a hammer coming to full cock is all that is necessary to put a bear on a bait into full flight. Big bears got to be big because they are cautious and leave the country at the least suspicious sound, smell, or motion. There are ways to get around the noisy, mechanical sound of cocking a rifle.

Do not sit in a blind with your rifle at full cock and capped. Set the hammer at full cock, but for safety reasons keep the cap off the nipple. When the time comes to shoot, place it on. It is best to use some sort of capping device, such as a spring-loaded capper (available from Michaels of Oregon, PO Box 13010, Portland, Oregon 97213) or one of the homemade leather jobs.

(You are asking for frustration if you try to put the cap on the nipple while a bear is just a few steps away. Those little metal tins the caps come in are designed to stay locked when you want them to open and to open when you want them locked. It is impossible to take out a single cap; you either get none, or all of them spill into the leaves!)

The use of some sort of quick-load device is also recommended. I used to make my own by gluing two plastic pill vials base-to-base. I would carry a premeasured powder charge in one and a bullet in the other. These homemade jobs worked OK. They were not very durable, though. Don't get the pill vials with the child-proof lids. They are also hunter-proof when a bear has your adrenaline up and you need another shot in a hurry. I have switched from my old homemade quick loaders to a commercially made device marketed by the Butler Creek Corporation, Jackson Hole, Wyoming 83001. These plastic quick loaders even have a place to carry caps.

I hear a lot of conversation about how muzzleloaders are not very dependable and produce a lot of misfires. The rifles don't produce misfires—the folks that load them do! A properly loaded muzzleloader is very dependable, even in wet weather.

First, wipe the bore clean of all excess oil. Any oil in the bore of a muzzleloader is excess. Use several dry patches, or you may want to wipe the bore first with a patch dampened with lighter fuel or iso-propyl alcohol. Either will serve as a solvent.

After every trace of oil has been removed and a dry patch comes out of the bore cleaner than it went in, you are ready to clear the passageway in the nipple. I do this by firing three caps on the nipple. This will blow out any oil or moisture that may have collected. It is very simple to check for an open passage. Just hold the muzzle near some leaves or grass and fire. If the nipple passage is open, a blast of air will jar the leaves or blades of grass.

When you are sure the bore is dry and the nipple open, pour in a premeasured powder charge. Tap the stock against the ground or rap the side of the barrel several times with the palm of your hand to make the powder settle in the chamber. Next, seat the ball firmly against the powder charge. Having an airspace between the powder and bullet is dangerous and may cause a blowup. Then place the cap on the nipple.

Muzzleloaders will shoot with dependability if they are properly loaded with precautions taken. My hunting partner, Dr. Oris Brannan, once knocked over a bear in the Rockies after sitting for over two hours in a hard driving rain with his .50-caliber Hawken tucked under his arm. I once went on a black powder hunt on St. Vincent's Island in the Gulf of Mexico and it rained very heavily right at the end of our trip. In our haste to break a sodden camp and get back to the mainland, I didn't fire the charge I had in my .54-caliber Jonathan Browning Mountain Rifle. I also didn't want to take the time for the thorough cleanup that must follow the firing of a black powder rifle. I removed the nipple and attached a red shipping label which read "This Gun Is Loaded" that I keep for such occasions. The gun was put in my gun locker and forgotten for nearly three months. I took it out to the range at my home, and it shot on the first try. That gun had been rained on and stored for several months and it still shot. I think this proves my point.

9

Hunting with Bow
and Arrow

If ever a big game animal was designed to provide optimum ex-citement for the archer, it is the black bear. The ubiquitous animal is usually within easy traveling distance of most bow hunters. Its popu-larity is evidenced by the large number of bear hunting guides and outfitters who cater to stick hunters. I have hunted with two guides in the Rockies who serve bow hunters and black powder hunters exclu-sively because, as they explained, hunters who use bows or muzzle-loaders are usually the best sportsmen, best hunters, and best shots. Even with their more primitive weapons, they lose fewer wounded animals because they don't take high-risk shots at game.

Hunting over a bait affords the archer the best chances of tagging a bruin. Because of the close range necessary for most archers to place an arrow precisely in a lethal spot, there is added excitement. Most guides have blinds or tree stands less than twenty feet from a bait. This may appear to be a little too close to a bow hunter who has never arrowed a bear. Believe me, this short range shooting is necessary for most hunters loosing an arrow at their first bear. If you think you got the shakes from "buck fever," just wait until you look at your first bear down the shaft of an arrow.

Gary Ginther, a guide in Colorado, once told me about a bow hunter client of his who missed a bear completely at nine feet. That hunter didn't just miss the makings of a bearskin rug; Gary told me that bear would probably have been the biggest bear ever killed with a bow! I respect Gary's judgement in this case since several of his clients have put bears in the Pope and Young record book. The archer was a good shot and was certainly capable of placing a broadhead through the chest of a whitetail at three times that distance, but a bear stimulates enormous gushings of adrenaline, and that makes it difficult to perform the smooth release necessary for accurate bow shooting.

If you know you will be hunting from a tree stand, schedule some serious prehunt practice sessions shooting from an elevated position. If nothing else is available, you can shoot down from the roof of your house or garage or down into a gully from a steep bank.

The successful bow hunter must possess the skills necessary to get within arrow range of a bear.

The best choice for tree stand practice is from a tree stand itself. I keep a Baker Platform Ladder tree stand set up on the mountain behind my house (Baker Mfg. Co., PO Box 1003, Valdosta, Georgia 31601). This convenient setup allows me to practice shooting from a tree stand on a regular basis year-round. I practice almost exclusively from a tree stand for my bear hunts when I know I will be hunting from an elevated tree stand.

I always take along my own portable tree stand when going on a bow hunt. A permanent tree stand that has been built by a guide may have some serious disadvantages. For example, if several previous clients have taken shots at or spooked a bear from that stand, you can bet that tree stand will be the first place a bear will look if he has discovered a human there on previous visits. I once shot a bear while sitting in a portable stand that was about forty yards away from a permanent stand where bears had discovered hunters before me. In this case, that empty stand was a decoy of sorts. That bear was so intent on scrutinizing that old stand that he never even looked in my direction.

Most guides place permanent tree stands so that prevailing winds will keep your odor away from the bait and the direction in which the bear usually approaches the bait. On one of my early bear hunts in Ontario, I was in a ground blind, and the wind would shift 180 degrees every twenty minutes or so. This inconsistent wind direction is typical of many bear hunting locations during spring hunts when the weather is frequently changing. I never saw a bear until the wind quit changing directions. A tree stand would have helped keep my scent above the ground and would have probably afforded me a shot.

Much of the black bear habitat is located on lands in national parks, wildlife refuges, and on land owned by timber companies. It is illegal to construct a tree stand on many federal refuges and national parks, but in many cases a portable tree stand is allowed. However, if you use nails to build a tree stand on timber company land, the nails will remain in the trunk of a tree long after the stand has rotted away. When that tree containing the nails is harvested, those nails can do severe damage to a chain saw or a saw in the lumber mill. Damaging a saw and possibly injuring a timber company employee is a pretty sorry way to say "thanks" for being allowed to hunt on a company's property!

No matter where you plan to use a tree stand, check the regulations very closely. Tree stand regulations can vary considerably within a

My friend Oak Duke, watching a bait from a tree stand. Oak is one of the few traditional bow hunters I know who still uses the classic long bow.

state, depending upon whether you are hunting on private, state, federal, or timber company property.

If you are bow hunting in an area that does not allow any hunting from a tree stand, then you will have to take measures to get close enough to a bear on the ground to place your arrow accurately. A blind of some sort is certainly advantageous to screen the human form and also to mask the motions necessary to bring a bow to the aiming position and pull it to full draw.

It is desirable to have the stand constructed well in advance of being occupied by the hunter. If it is, any bears visiting that bait will have a chance to get used to it, and they will become less conscious of it in time.

The biggest handicap of the bow hunter is not the possibility of being seen by a bear. There are some hunters who are convinced a bear has poor eyesight. I am not so sure. I would agree his eyes don't measure up to his nose, but I have been spotted by bears on several occasions when I was downwind and motionless.

The greatest risk of discovery by your quarry is that of being smelled by the excellent nose a bear possesses.

The most obvious technique to avoid this is to stay downwind. This should be obvious to anyone who has ever read at least one outdoor magazine from cover to cover. Unfortunately, there is only one drawback: to keep a bear upwind, you first have to know where the bear is!

If you are hunting from a stand, you can anticipate which direction the bruin will be traveling based upon signs you have read. Bears have been known to deviate from previous travel routes and schedules. They are not as regular in their travel routes and schedules as, say, whitetail deer. A whitetail will usually spend his entire life in a one-half square mile area and follow the same routes to feeding and bedding areas on a schedule you can almost set your watch by, whereas a bear will travel over twenty miles in a day foraging for food. He may leave a berry patch or a bait and not be back for a week.

Because of these erratic habits it is difficult to always anticipate accurately just when a bear will come within bow range and which direction he will come from.

To avoid being scented by a bear that approaches from a downwind angle, experienced bow hunters use one of several techniques. I have already mentioned getting up in a tree stand to help disperse your human perfume above ground level. Since much of our bear habitat in North America is in mountains, the hunter who waits in a tree stand or in a blind on the ground must take thermal winds into consideration when making tactical decisions about where to place a tree stand or blind.

Thermal winds are created on still, windless days at dawn and dusk. As the morning sun warms the night air, it expands and begins to rise in a very gentle, almost undiscernable drift. About the only way you can detect a thermal wind is with smoke from a cigarette or pipe.

In the evenings the air cools as the sun goes down, and then condenses, and drifts toward the ground. When I first learned of thermal winds, I could never remember which way they went at different times of the day. An easy way is to just remember that the air on calm, windless days moves the same way as the sun. As the sun moves up in the morning, so does the air. As the sun goes down, the air does likewise.

Let me emphasize that thermals only need be of concern to the bow hunter when he is hunting on a slope on a calm, windless day. Thermal drifts are usually so gentle that they are dispersed by the gusty winds of a weather front or strong prevailing winds.

It is a good idea to have a stand or blind both above and below a bait or area you are watching so you can position yourself either above or below the bait as thermal direction dictates.

In addition to placing yourself above the range of a bear's nose, you may use a commercial or improvised scent to mask your odor. The commercial varieties are marketed primarily for deer hunters, but they can be useful to bear hunters also. In areas where skunks are native inhabitants, a skunk scent would be a good choice. I guarantee a few drops of a commercial skunk scent sprinkled around your stand or blind will eliminate just about any possibility of a bear smelling you. A word of advice: don't put the essence of skunk on your body or clothes unless you choose to be ostracized from your hunting camp or home for a considerable time span. Sprinkle the scent around your stand or blind. Use one of those little sponges that come on some bow quivers, cup up a dish sponge and attach it to your bow, or keep the

Most bears taken by bow hunters are shot at close range over baits. Many outfitters and black bear guides specialize in bow hunting and build blinds just a few steps away from baits to provide precise arrow placement at ultra close range.

scent in a small air tight container and open the container when you want to be surrounded by the aroma.

BOWS FOR BEARS

It would be easy at this point to go into a lengthy dissertation including brand names, bow designs, and other trivia. I'll keep my comments brief. For hunting black bears I use a Brown Bear (Bear Archery Company) compound bow set at sixty-five pounds draw weight. Bear Archery sent me the bow for field testing, and as I was unpacking it in the living room, my wife went nuts over the beautiful laminated wood. She is very fond of antique furniture and knows good wood when she sees it. I agreed that it was a beautiful bow. But she nearly had a stroke when I began to wrap the entire bow with camouflage tape. Even after I explained why the bow had to be completely camouflaged, she still thought I was mentally deficient for covering up that good-looking wood with drab old camo tape.

Attached to my bow is a bow quiver (yes, it has a cover over the broadheads). I also have silencers on the strings. Near the arrow rest I have an arrow holder which holds the arrow in position until I draw the arrow, then it releases and flips out of the way. Your left hand can become mighty tired and cramped after you hold an arrow in place for several hours waiting for a bear to show up.

A bear has thick, woolly fur and usually several inches of fat between the fur and hide. Neither the fur nor the fat helps to leave a substantial blood trail for tracking. A bear will eventually begin to leave a blood trail if you got a good hit, but those first few hundred yards can be devilish to work out. Because of this, I have a Kolpin "Sure Track" string tracker attached to my bow. This is merely a small container which holds 300 yards of highly visible blaze orange nylon thread. To use it, just strip out a few yards of thread and attach it to your broadhead. When you arrow a bear and he takes off, he pulls the nylon thread after him, leaving a trail that could be followed by even a nearsighted green horn.

Since I always have to have cameras along on my hunts, I carry a camouflage day pack with a few accessories. My check list for an archery bear hunt includes: a drag rope, camo face paint, insect head net and bug repellant (an absolute must for spring bear hunts in Canada, Alaska, and northern United States), broadhead sharpener, pliers, extra bow string, assorted scents, knife, waterproof matches, compass, area map, flashlight and toilet paper. Aside from the more obvious use, sheets of toilet paper are ideal for marking blood sign when tracking a bear. Just drop a sheet on each drop of blood, then if you lose the trail, you can just look back over your shoulder and the row of toilet paper will point in the last known direction the bear was traveling. You can then focus your attention on and search for the trail in that direction.

I have frequently crossed trails with other bow hunters who preferred the old-style two-edge broadhead rather than one of the newer heads with four or more cutting edges. Their contention was that the two-edge blade gave deeper penetration than a four-edge on the ample bulk of a heavyweight bear. I would not argue that point. But I do believe that the blade with four cutting edges is a better choice for hunting bears since you are more likely to cut major blood vessels with four edges as compared to a blade with only the two cutting edges of the single bladed models. I also contend that the blades of a broadhead should be at least one-inch wide.

There are several theories on what type of edge a broadhead should have. Some well-known experienced archers prefer the immaculately honed razor edge of a surgeon's scalpel. Others opt for the rough or saw-tooth edge. My personal choice for bears is the saw-tooth edge. The razor edge is more prone to damage if it strikes a bone, whereas the saw-tooth edge will bounce off or graze a bone and still retain some of its cutting ability. The main reason I use the saw-tooth edge on my broadheads is because it is the type of edge butchers put on their butcher knives. A broadhead kills by causing massive hemorrhaging (the result of tissue being cut). I will accept the choice of a professional butcher as to which edge cuts meat best.

In the chapters on shooting bears with a rifle, I strongly recommend placing your shot in a location that would break the spine and one or both shoulders. The bow hunter's weapon does not have that capability. A shoulder shot that hits the massive femur of a larger than average bear may have the same effect as hitting that bear with a half-pound of your favorite instant pudding.

Gary Ginther, one of the best bow hunters I have ever been with, is a professional guide who has killed many bears himself and guided numerous bow hunting clients to a bear skin rug. Gary once shot a bear a little too far forward and hit the large bone in the upper foreleg. He was shooting a recurve bow with a draw weight of over seventy pounds at a distance of about nine paces. The arrow hit the foreleg and bounced straight back! I killed that same bear later (we were able to recognize it because of a massive facial injury), and when we skinned it, we looked for the scar from Gary's shot. Right where he called his shot we found a scar shaped like this " + " where his arrow had entered.

The best shot for the bow hunter is an angling shot that will enter behind the ribs on the near side, pass through the lungs, and exit somewhere in the forward section of the rib cage on the far side. Or, if conditions are not favorable for that shot, the next best choice is hitting a bear right behind the shoulder, passing through the lungs, and exiting just behind the rib cage on the far side.

You can spend a lot of time waiting for a bear to accidentally position himself for one of these shots. In fact, a bear may come to a bait and then leave without ever offering a shot like I described. You can increase your chances of getting an ideal shot several ways. Rather than put your bait in one big pile, or use large chunks of bait that a bear can run off with and eat in thick cover or out of the archer's range,

This is the best angle for a bow hunter to take a shot. The arrow should enter behind the last rib and angle forward into the chest cavity for maximum hemorrhaging. (Photo courtesy of Arkansas Game and Fish Department)

cut the bait into fairly small pieces and scatter some of it around. As the bear moves around collecting the scattered tidbits, you will probably have several opportunities for a raking lung shot.

Another alternative is putting the bait under some heavy logs, which will cause the bear to move around in the process of uncovering the bait. You may want to build a cubby like those used by trappers. A cubby looks like the corner of an old-style split rail fence. The bear will have to stand at the entrance of the cubby and stick his head in to get the bait, which will put him in position for an effective shot.

In theory, these techniques sound very effective. But in actual practice, they can be nerve racking. Wait until you have been perched in a tree stand for about twenty minutes waiting for a bear to get into position for a shot. Since most bears are shot by bow hunters at a range of between twenty-five and fifty feet, this close proximity adds to a severe case of "bear fever." Waiting for that perfect shot to present itself has to be just about the most exciting thing that can happen to a bow hunter in the outdoors.

One of the major keys to bow hunting success is the ability of the archer to place *that first shot* accurately. I speak at a lot of sportsmen's clubs as a regular program and also as an after-dinner speaker at annual banquets, and I frequently ask the audience how much they practice before bow hunts. Most of them start too late before the hunt starts, but the most common error among archery hunters is the procedure they use in their practice sessions. The vast majority will put up a target, walk off to a known distance, and then stand in that one spot and lose a dozen arrows. They shoot arrows like the old time artillery gunners used to shell the enemy: you fire one round and then make adjustments to walk your projectiles onto target. When you stand in one spot and shoot a dozen arrows, did you ever notice how much tighter your group gets as you get down to the last few arrows? But you won't get a half dozen shots at a bear to "walk" your arrows onto the target. You will get one shot—if you are lucky!

Practice sessions should be set up to simulate real hunting conditions as much as possible. *Never* do all your shooting on a clean-cut field from the same distance at ground level. And don't do all your shooting on ground level. If you shoot either up or down a steep slope, there will be a significant change in the trajectory of your arrow. The only way to learn to shoot uphill, downhill, out of a tree stand, out of a ground blind, and in between trees is to practice under those same conditions. Take one shot and one shot only and then move to another location. Moving on every shot will increase your ability to make that first shot count. The first one is usually the only one that counts in bow hunting.

BROWNS AND GRIZZLIES WITH A BOW

Of the one million-plus bow hunters in this country, I doubt if more than forty or fifty of them have taken a grizzly or brown bear with a bow. Hunting the big bears with a bow is not for everyone. It is not a good idea to even consider it unless you have hunted many years with a bow and have several black bears to your credit.

You can expect to spend about $2,500 for one of the less expensive trips and above $6,500 for all the others. Most guided trips will fall into the latter category. Also, you should ask any potential grizzly or brown bear guide for a list of bow hunting references. You should also let him know what your maximum-range shooting ability is.

It is foolish to release an arrow at a grizzly or brown bear without having someone right next to you with a high-powered backup rifle. Death by massive hemorrhaging will take more time than a bear needs to eat your giblets.

Because of the tremendous body mass of the big bears, I would recommend the heaviest bow you can shoot accurately. If you can't manage a bow of sixty pounds pull or better, I strongly urge you to stick to black bears.

BOW HUNTING WITH DOGS

Many archers opt to hunt bruins behind a pack of dogs. This technique is probably second only to hunting over a bait for effectiveness. A pack of hounds at full cry chasing a bear is one of the best ways I know to field-test your body's ability to produce adrenaline. This excitement is increased when you know that when the bear is finally treed, all you will have to bring the bruin to earth is a handful of sharp sticks.

It is of the utmost importance that you keep your arrows in a quiver that holds your arrows firmly and also covers the broadheads. A bear chase is a frantic race to keep the dogs in hearing and then a final dash to get to the melee at the site where the bear either trees or turns to fight the dogs. It is very easy for an archer to cause himself serious injury with his own arrows in the excitement of a bear chase.

Even if you plan to hunt from horseback, get your legs and lungs in tip-top shape before you go because a bear will often be treed in country so rugged you cannot ride a horse into the fracas. I strongly urge you to also spend a lot of time on a horse before you go out west for a bear hunt with dogs. When you spend a day on horseback and haven't prepared or toughened your posterior, you won't be able to walk or sit for days. Go to a stable and rent a horse until you can stay aboard for several hours without any ill effects. It is the best trip insurance you can have if you plan to hunt on horseback.

10

Hunting Over Baits

There are some who are quick to condemn the hunting of bears over a bait as being unsportsmanlike. There was a time that I felt the same way.

A wild bear does not come into a bait like a panhandler bear comes into a garbage dump at a campground. He possesses a wariness and alertness that exceeds the caution of a ten-point buck checking a ground scrape. A bear will often stay out of sight and watch a bait for an hour or more. He will circle the bait in an effort to detect some strange scent. If he hears the least sound, he will be off for the tall and uncut.

Many bear hunters are unsuccessful because they cannot sit still in a blind or up in a tree stand. To be still, you have to enjoy a reasonable degree of comfort. Dress warmly. Make yourself a comfortable seat. Protect yourself from insects. Try to anticipate anything that might cause you to move about or be restless. And don't smoke.

Earlier in my career as a hunter I got really cold on a deer stand.

If you put on a scent such as anise extract, sardine oil, bacon grease, or a commercial preparation like Bear Power, it will distract a bear and help mask your human odor when you are on stand or watching a bait.

I swore I would never be cold on a stand again and I haven't! I always wear more clothes than I need. If you overdress, you can take a layer or two off. Wear a warm head covering since most of your body heat is lost through the head and neck.

A good set of wool or quilted underwear under camouflage-insulated coveralls does a good job. Warm gloves and insulated boots top off the wardrobe. Don't forget rain gear; my preference for sitting over a bait in the rain is a camouflage rain suit. Check the regulations before going out of state to hunt as many states and provinces require special outer clothing. (A good example is Manitoba, which requires white clothing.)

Wherever it is legal, I like camouflage clothing for sitting on a blind or in a tree stand. If you are hunting in the fall, a camo pattern that is predominantly brown like that used by duck hunters would be a good choice. If it is a spring hunt, then a dominant green would be a good choice. If you are hunting strange territory, ask your outfitter for some suggestions on clothing.

A tree stand will get you and your scent above a bear's normal line of vision and help keep your scent above his supersensitive nose.

Hunting over a bait is most effective during the spring. But spring is also the season when the black flies are at their worst in the north country. In other, more warm climates, mosquitoes will be taking a crack at you. Head nets, gloves, long-sleeve shirts with tight-fitting cuffs, pants cuffs tucked into your boots, and generous applications of bug dope are necessary if you want to spend your time shooting bears rather than swatting at man-eating bugs.

A bait should always be checked and worked as quietly as possible. Most experienced bear baiters check their baits late in the morning to avoid coming up on a bear that is on the bait feeding and spooking him off. A spooked bear will be a long time coming back, if ever. This is especially true of big bears.

I have a bear rug about two steps away from where I am writing. It's there because I approached a bait from the downwind side and surprised a bear. It was late afternoon, and I really didn't expect a bear to be on the bait until right at dark. More from habit than anything else, I sneaked up on the bait and got a shot. It was the only shot I got on that long, expensive trip.

My Canadian bear hunting partner, John Long, taught me the importance of being quiet on a bait, coming in from downwind and ready to shoot. Whenever John and I work a bait, we not only go in on the sneak, but one of us also keeps an eye out while the other freshens up the bait and reads for sign. It is common for a bear to claim a bait station as his own personal private property and stay close to protect his find. If he hears the sounds of something fooling around the bait, he may think it is a rival bear and come at it fast and loud to scare off the intruder.

I don't rule out the possibility that a black bear would attack a hunter who was working a bait, but I don't think the odds are very high. If you have a bait in grizzly country, then your chances of getting searched by a griz that has claimed a bait are pretty good.

One of us stands ready with a rifle while working a black bear bait to be ready for a shot if a bear does come to inspect the disturbance at a bait. You can bet that blackie is going to be leaving the country when he discovers just what species of varmint is fooling around his groceries. You won't have time to fumble for a rifle and get off a shot. If you aren't ready for those surprise visits while working a bait, then you will never reap the benefits.

The location for a bait station takes a lot of consideration. Obviously, there must be bears in the area. Other considerations are not quite so obvious. Is there a blind location on the downwind side of the bait? Are there alternate locations for blinds in other directions if the wind shifts? Is there thick cover nearby? (Bears don't like to travel far from cover.) Is the bait likely to be found by other hunters? Is it fairly easy to haul bait to? Is it positioned to get early afternoon shade? (In warm weather, bears will come to a shade bait earlier in the afternoon.)

A portable tree stand, like the Baker shown here, allows the hunter to move to a tree on the downwide side of a bait if the wind shifts. A permanent tree stand does not permit that option.

There are many indicators which reveal the presence of bears in an area. Your state game and fish commission can give you some help in where to get started. It is also a very good idea to ask for specific regulations on baiting bears. These regulations vary from state to state, and many reflect some real creative thinking! Some states specify exactly what can be used on a bait, where and when they can be placed, and, in some cases, require that they be identified or even registered.

One of the topics that always comes up when bear hunters get together is what are the best bear baits. Just about every bear hunter has his own special combination. If there is a common thread running through all the "favorite" bear baits, it would have to be that, invariably, the baits consisted of a mix of several different things. The combinations include honey, ham scraps, bacon grease, sardines, fish, candy, pastry, chicken, beef scraps, pork scraps, produce trimmings, apples, and peanut butter, just to name a few. I have a friend in Canada who even gets trappers to save beaver carcasses for spring bear baits.

One of the things to consider when putting out a bear bait is the volume in which you can secure bait. Grocery stores are good sources for meat scraps and vegetable trimmings. Restaurants are good sources for scraps and bacon grease. Don't overlook school or institutional cafeterias as a source of bacon grease and food scraps. One restaurant near the Great Smoky Mountains National Park supplies all the ham scraps used by the many biologists who trap bears for research.

Farms and orchards are good sources for produce that are not suitable for sale but very suitable for bear consumption. A good friend who has an apple orchard gives me all the apples I want to pick up. (After they fall off the tree, they get spots on them and he cannot sell them.)

Some sort of sweet adds to the popularity of a bear bait and should be included in your recipe mix. John Long once got nearly a ton (that is not a misprint) of honey that had crystallized just for the price of the jars. That honey sweetened a lot of bear baits. I have some hunting buddies in Colorado who make several trips a year to a big candy factory and buy candy in fifty-five gallon drums. The candy they buy is waste candy that the company cannot sell. It is dirt cheap. A "day old" bakery shop is a good place to pick up old pastry to sweeten a bear bait.

Fish is another component I consider important to a good bear bait. They don't always eat the fish, but I think the odor helps attract

Bear hunters "freshen" a bait with honey, bacon grease, fish, and meat scraps.

them. I have another friend who runs a trout farm. During the heat of late summer he loses a lot of trout while transporting them. He throws them in the freezer for me, and I go by every once in a while and pick up a load.

After hunting bears and working baits in many parts of the country, I have noticed the two key ingredients in all the successful ones are variety and bounty. The more bait you put on a station, the better it will produce, and variety definitely adds to a bait's appeal. However, two cans of sardines and a jar of honey dumped in the woods yesterday afternoon do not a bear bait make. A bear bait that is worth sitting over requires a lot of scouting, a lot of bait hauling on a regular basis, and a lot of patience. Anyone who kills a bear on a bait that he has prepared and worked himself has earned that bear! Because it does take so long and so much work, to say nothing of the logistics required to keep a steady flow of bait coming in, most bear hunters hire guides who have several active baits for their clients.

In addition to edible foodstuffs, some savvy guides add something

John Long checks a bait in Ontario that has been "hit" by a bear.

to the bait pile for aromatic purposes only. I have a bear hunting partner who buys anise extract by the case at the supermarket. Every time he works a bait he splashes some on the surrounding brush and tree trunks. When he sits on a blind near one of his baits, he liberally sprinkles it around his blind to mask his scent. (It is so simple it is genius.) The anise scent is very strong. It smells good to a bear, and he is familiar with the scent because he smells it everytime he comes to the bait.

The folks at Skunks Unlimited, Rt. 4 Box 85, Cumberland, Wisconsin 54829, make a commercial scent called Bear Power. I have used this, and I am quite pleased with the results. I have had bears literally destroy a rotten log where I had sprinkled Bear Power. It is also not a bad idea to sprinkle around some of the insect repellant you will be using so any bears coming to that bait will be familiar with the scent.

Many biologists and bear hunters attract bears to a bait by cooking meat scraps or burning honey. Meat scraps can be cooked up quite nicely with a small butane torch. Just place the meat in a coffee can or hold it on a stick. Ham scraps give off a very inviting odor when seared with a torch.

Bait should be placed so that it cannot be hauled off by small predators, stray dogs, or scavengers. One method calls for hanging the goodies up off the ground out of reach of small varmints. I believe that hanging the bait also increases the airborne aroma which is critical to attracting bears. Burlap bags are ideal for hanging bear baits.

Some hunters put the bait in piles on the ground and cover it with logs and limbs. This is not a bad method since it will take the bear some time and maneuvering to get under the logs, giving the hunter several opportunities for a good shot.

It is good practice not to put large pieces of bait on a station. A bear will take the large chunk and run into thick cover to eat it, affording little opportunity for a shot. Bears are especially prone to take a big chunk of bait and run if several bears are hitting the same bait. They go to cover with a chunk of bait to avoid some rival taking it away from them.

In some cases bears discover the hunter before he can take a shot. Many people who hunt over a bait for the first time miss their chance because they erroneously assumed the bear was going to casually stroll up to the bait and begin to feed without even looking around. Don't believe it! If several bears are coming into a bait, you can bet there have been bear-to-bear confrontations and they are going to be on the lookout for rivals. They may have spotted or even been shot at by another hunter on that same station previously.

I have a standard rule for myself when hunting over a bait with a rifle: take the first decent shot offered. Keep your rifle ready for easy access. Don't hang it up on a limb or prop it behind you for the sake of being comfortable. The more moving you have to do to take a shot, the less your chances of success. As soon as the bear is in your effective range, take him—he may not get any closer. I have heard many sad tales about hunters thinking a baited bear was like a fish in a barrel. (A lot more bears come to baits than go to the taxidermist.)

When I am bow hunting, I like to place a shot just behind the last rib, angling toward the shoulder on the far side. This allows my arrow to do maximum damage and insure a kill. Because of the limited range of a bow, I have to wait for the bear to work in real close before I shoot. That is why I think bow hunting over a bait is just about the most exciting form of bear hunting I know.

A portable tree stand is a valuable asset for the hunter who sits over a bear bait. Most blinds or stands are placed downwind from the prevailing wind direction. Sometimes a storm front will cause a wind shift and put you on the upwind side of a bait. Then you might as well be hunting bears at home plate in Yankee Stadium. A portable tree stand allows you to move yourself to the downwind side and be back in business. A portable tree stand also offers a tactical advantage when a bear has somehow discovered you in a permanent tree stand or ground blind. Everytime he comes to that bait, he is going to be looking for trouble in that location. A permanent tree stand can be a pretty effective decoy if it is empty and you are located someplace else. This will work occasionally, but a spooked bear won't usually come back. There are just enough exceptions to make it worthwhile.

Whether you are freshening a bait, or coming in to hunt over it, you should always approach that bait as if there was a bear on it. Come from downwind, come sneaking very slow, come looking, and come ready to shoot.

11

Hunting With Hounds

From the dense conifers of northern California, to the mountains of western North Carolina, hound music has thrilled bear hunters. There are few things in life like the bellowing of bear hounds who have just gotten a snootful of fresh bear scent. It is a brand of music that is infectious and stimulates old bones, muscles, and lungs to travel distances and climb heights their owner never thought possible.

Many of the men who raise bear hounds care more about the chase than the kill. In fact, most of the dedicated hunters only carry a rifle to protect their dogs. If a bear is treed, most of the time the dog handler will put his dogs on a leash and leave the bear high in a tree wondering what all the commotion was about.

A bear race (as the hound men call a chase) may last only a few hundred yards or into the next day. Most races will fall somewhere between these two extremes, with a chase lasting several hours. Those several hours can seem like several lifetimes depending on how you

This bear and hound encounter in western North Carolina is typical of the excitement that can occur when bears and dogs meet in some secluded thicket in the mountains. (Photo by Joel Arrington)

are following the dogs. In some places it is possible to keep the dogs within hearing range with four-wheel-drive vehicles. In some areas you can follow the biggest part of the chase on horseback. But no matter what method of transportation you use at the beginning, bears have a way of running through terrain so thick, steep, or rugged that the hunter ends up on foot.

This is one type of bear hunting where your legs and lungs had better be in shape. I went on a hound hunt in western North Carolina near Robbinsville and thought I was in pretty good shape until I started following those mountaineers around those steep slopes. Then I realized that in all my forty-two years I had never really been tired. Oh, I thought I had known exhaustion back in college when I had run track and played linebacker on the football team. I didn't. I was stepping on my tongue, and my lungs felt like they were about the size of hickory nuts as I tried to keep up with dogs and those old mountain boys.

Shots at treed bears can range from close and easy to long and difficult (such as through the dense foliage of a tall tree). (Photo by Joel Arrington)

Remember, there are no absolutes when it comes to predicting bear behavior. What a bear will do when a pack of baying hounds gets on his tail is no exception to that rule. However, younger, leaner bears will make longer runs before they tree or turn to beat up on the dogs. An old heavy weight bear is like a defensive tackle—big, powerful, but not built for long-distance running. An older bear is more apt to lose patience and turn on a pack of hounds. (If you really want to see a hound owner travel, let a bear wade into his dogs!)

There have been situations where dogs have killed a mature bear in a fight, but most of the episodes I have heard about ended up the other way. A lot more dogs are done in by a bear who got tired of hearing them bark. Most bear–dog fights end with the hunter arriving to shoot the bear.

When a bear is treed, a dog handler will try to catch up to his dogs before the bear is shot. A wounded bear that falls into a pack of dogs waiting on the ground can run up a very expensive dog replacement bill with just a few swipes or chomps. (A good bear dog starts off at a price of about a thousand bucks, and the cost rises steeply after that.)

Since the shots are not long, you don't need a long-barreled scope-sighted rifle weighing nine pounds. Take my advice: travel light. You will do a lot more toting than you will shooting, so I suggest a short-barreled bolt-action with open sights or, if possible, a lever action chambered for something with a little more punch than a .30-30. Many of the old time southern Appalachian bear hunters I know use .44 magnum handguns, .35 Remington .30-06 autoloaders, .45-70 Marlin lever actions and, of course, the venerable old model 94 in .30-30 caliber. On my most recent bear hunt with those southern mountaineers, they were pretty interested in a big-bore 94 chambered for the .375 Winchester I was packing.

On one of my hunts in the Smokies, we had treed a bear that was really man shy. Every time we approached the tree, that old bear would jump and run. After a jump or two, one of the young mountain boys (whom I suspect was part deer; he even got ahead of the hounds a time or two) got close enough for a shot. He was using an old surplus 6.5 Japanese rifle. His shot killed the bear so quickly that the bear didn't even tumble out of the tree. He died right in the fork where he was perched without even so much as a quiver.

As we dressed the bear, we performed an amateur autopsy since I was curious as to where he had hit that bear to kill it so quickly. As soon as I saw the entrance wound, I knew why. The bullet hole was not round but shaped like a short stub of a pencil that was about an inch and a half long. The bullet had hit the bear in a broadside position instead of end first. The rifling on that old 6.5 had long ago either been worn out or rusted out, so the bullet didn't spin in flight; it tumbled end over end. It is not the most accurate shot, but it will deliver a terrible whack when it hits the target broadside!

Hound hunting is probably the best way to collect a bear rug. In areas where bears are plentiful, a pack of hounds will produce the highest success ratio, with hunting over a bait the second most productive.

Bear hunting regulations probably vary more from state to state than any other form of game animal. The following states allow hunting with hounds: Alaska, Arizona, California, Colorado, Florida, Idaho, Maine, Massachusetts, Michigan, Minnesota, New Hampshire, New Mexico, New York, North Carolina, South Carolina, Tennessee, Utah, Virginia, West Virginia, Wisconsin. Check the regulations before turn-

Most bear dog packs are a mixture of several breeds like this one in western North Carolina. (Photo by Joel Arrington)

ing your hounds loose because most states have restrictions on pack size, pack registration, areas and dates closed to hounds, and other regulations.

Only three Canadian provinces allow the hunting of black bears with dogs: British Columbia, Ontario, and Quebec.

Good bear dogs are hard to come by. You can't stroll down to the neighborhood sports emporium and pick up a six-pack of bear hounds. One of the few folks I know of who has bear dogs for sale in any appreciable numbers is one of my old bear chasing partners in western North Carolina, Roy Wilson, Route 1, Box 288, Robbinsville, North Carolina 28771. Roy provides the bear hounds for Blue Boar Lodge in Robbinsville.

(While I am on the subject, the Blue Boar Lodge offers a unique and economic three-day bear hunting package. It costs less than the tab for staying in a moderately priced motel for the same period of time, and you will get bear hunting and some of the best food you have

It's dawn at Wolf Pen Gap in western North Carolina, and these dogs are about to be released on a bear hunt in the Great Smoky Mountains.

ever eaten thrown in. When I was last at the lodge, the three-day package was only $150. They take about twenty hunters at a time, and you have the choice of being on stand or following the dogs. May I suggest taking a stand? The bear country in western North Carolina is the roughest I have ever been in. A hunt with hounds in the Rocky Mountains is not a bad choice either. It combines the excitement of the hunt with some of the most fantastic scenery a man will ever see. I have yet to view a single unattractive spot in the Rockies!)

It is possible to raise and train your own bear dogs. But you would have to work at it full time, live close enough to bear country to have some bears to train them on, and have about ten or fifteen years of bear hunting experience so you will know more than the dogs you are trying to train.

A pack of good bear dogs must possess various skills. There must be a dog or two that has a good cold nose and be able to track a bear on a scent that is less than steaming hot. There must be dogs in the pack with speed and stamina to catch up with the bear and force him to tree or turn and fight on the ground. In the case of the latter, you better have a few dogs that are aggressive enough to jump a bear that has chosen to stand his ground and fight. A dog doesn't live long if he is long on guts and short in brains. A dog must be brave enough to fight, but he must also exercise some judgment as to when and where to bite a bear.

The once or twice a year bear hunter who wants to hunt with dogs will come out way ahead in time and money spent if he will get a guide that uses dogs or else recruit some bear hunting buddies who have dogs. (I usually take along about a hundred pounds of dried dog food

These strike dogs seem to be yelling, "Hey, Boss! A bear crossed the road right here!"
The pooches belong to Roy Wilson, one of the better known trainers who works out of
Blue Boar Lodge in Robbinsville, North Carolina.

when I hunt as a guest of another hunter who keeps a pack of bear hounds.)

It would be difficult, if not impossible, to describe a typical bear hunt behind hounds. When you have the action being determined in equal parts by a bear and a pack of highly excited bear hounds, anything can happen and usually does. Hunting bears with dogs is *not* merely a case of turning some dogs loose and then shooting a bear out of a tree!

Dogs are put onto fresh bear scent in one of several ways. In the West, where there are no roads, a pack of hounds is followed on horse back as the hounds course back and forth. If roads for four-wheel-drive vehicles are available, then a strike dog or two will be placed on a special carpet-covered plywood platform attached to the hood of a 4 × 4 jeep or truck. These dogs have super sensitive noses and can pick up a fresh bear scent while riding on the hood!

In places where both baiting and dog hunting is allowed, a hunter may put out several baits and check them on the morning of a hunt.

These bear hounds and hunters show the fatigue resulting from a typical long, hard chase in the steep, rugged terrain of the southern Appalachian Mountains. (Photo courtesy of Tennessee Wildlife Resources Agency)

If there are fresh signs—indication that a bear has recently hit the bait—then the dogs are turned loose and the chase is on.

Even though a pack of good hounds is on a fresh scent, a lot of things can happen that will allow the bear to escape. A short-tempered boar may only run a mile or so and then turn on the dogs and kill, maul or whip every pooch in the posse. Or you may get one of those bears that will run like crazy for several hours then climb a tree and rest while the dogs are running around below in a frenzy. When the hunters approach, the bear will jump to the ground and take off on another four- or five-mile sprint. He'll rest up again while the hunters catch up, and off he goes again until you run out of daylight, lose contact with the pack or just tucker out.

12

Stalking One on One

The black bear is probably the toughest animal in North America to stalk hunt one-on-one without bait or dogs. I have sneaked up on hundreds of deer, dozens of wild turkeys, and just about any other varmint in North America in fur or feathers. But the shy, retiring black bear favors the security of dense forest cover.

It doesn't take much of an outdoorsman to locate a heavily traveled deer route and sit nearby until a deer comes by since a deer will spend his life within one-half a square mile of where he was born. Deer will travel deer trails on the average of twice a day, going to and from feeding and bedding areas.

A black bear doesn't leave the obvious tracks of the whitetail deer. A black bear may travel a range over twenty square miles and may come through an area where you have found sign only once every three or four days. When he does pass by an area you may be watching, then he will probably do it in the dark.

A black bear is a very wary, secretive animal that keeps a low profile in the dense cover where he prefers to live. It is very difficult to get within rifle range of a black bear in eastern cover without the aid of dogs or bait.

Large numbers of black bears are killed each year by deer hunters. But in most cases their hunting luck was not any more attributable to skill than is winning a lottery. They just happen to be at the right place at the right time. I have talked to several dozen deer hunters who accidentally killed a black bear in one of our state managed public hunting areas. Without exception, the bear was spooked by a hunter and ran by the guy sitting on a stand, who dumped him.

The odds of getting up in the morning and saying to yourself, "Today I am going out and shoot a black bear!" and then doing it are about as good as me winning the Miss America pageant. However, there are a few things you can do to tip them a little bit more in your direction.

You will need to do a lot of scouting. These early scouting trips should be based upon where the state or province says there are good bear populations. Many hunters just take off willy-nilly to any patch of woods without ever asking the folks who study bears on a year-round basis where the bears are. A simple letter or phone call will save you a lot of fruitless miles in the bush.

Pick several areas from the list provided by the game and fish biologists and plan to scout each of the ones that are within a reasonable distance of your home. Bears leave a variety of signs, including scats, tracks, marked trees, and signs of feeding.

Bear scats can tell you a lot more than the mere fact that a bear has been in the area. More importantly, it can tell you what the bear has been eating, which can lead you to where he is feeding. Bear scats that are full of blueberry seeds should shout loud and clear that you should be working the blueberry patches.

In late summer, bears in the southern Appalachians will climb oak trees and break the tips off the limbs to get at immature acorns that have not fallen to the ground. These broken limbs are not hard to spot if you are observant enough to frequently check overhead foliage.

I have heard that a bear's nose is so good that he will only turn

The claw marks on this tree in northern Canada, as well as other bear sign in the area, indicate that it is a good place to hunt.

over those logs or rocks that have grubs, insects, or salamanders under them. I don't know if this is true or not, but I have seen hillsides in the Appalachians where an area half as large as a football field has had every rock turned over by a bear hunting groceries. It is not unusual to spot a rotten log that a bear has rolled over or drug out of position in search of food.

Male bears like to claw trees. These claw marks are highly visible signs of bear presence in an area. They are usually about head high on a man. These marked trees will often have chunks of bark about the size of a man's fist bitten out of them. Most biologists agree that most of these trees are marked during the breeding season in summer.

Bears will dig up yellow jacket nests to get at the larvae. This affection for grubs is evidenced in the fact that when a bear raids a domestic bee hive, he eats the bee larvae in addition to the honey.

Bear tracks are a little harder to see than deer tracks. The wide, soft pads on a bear's feet do not lend themselves to making sharp, easily defined tracks. About the only place you will be able to detect a bear track is in soft soil, mud, or sand. I have seen places in the Rockies where a bear would put his feet in exactly the same spots as he made a sharp turn around a large rock or traversed some particularly rough terrain. Distinct, individual tracks were not visible—only flattened-out leaves and other vegetation in a series of small spaces about the size of a man's hand. If a bear guide hadn't shown me the marks, I would never have noticed them on my own.

(Once when I was deep in the Great Smoky Mountains doing field work with some wildlife biologists who were doing a study of bear habitat utilization, we were using snares to capture bears so we could put radio collars on them. A lady biologist who was setting snares would actually get down on all fours to simulate where the bear would put each paw as it walked into a bait cubby or around some natural obstacle to reach a bait. She caught more than her share of bears.)

Anytime you are walking through rough country or around some natural obstacle, look for the pattern of flattened vegetation where bears have negotiated the area. This pattern of footprints—foot depressions might be a better term—is very common and easy to spot if you train yourself to look for them. This type of sign is often easier to locate in a heavily wooded area which black bears prefer than a clean track in soft soil.

There is an old saying: "When a pine needle falls out of a tree, a

Winter kill sites are good places to ambush a bear. Brian Spencer, famous hockey player for the Buffalo Sabres, checks for fresh bear sign near the carcass of this moose that was struck by a train in northern Ontario.

turkey will see it fall, a deer will hear it hit the ground, and a bear will smell it hit the ground.'' It's the truth. Because of a bear's excellent nose, you have absolutely no chance to get a shot at a bear that is downwind from you. The noise of a hunter moving slowly through the woods won't usually send a bear running. He hears noises in the woods all the time. If you wear camouflage and use available cover to screen your movements and break up your silhouette, then a bear probably won't see you.

You must always remember that a bear can smell you from a long distance away. Hunt accordingly or you will never get a shot. Always hunt either into the wind or at a right angle to avoid being scented. (Photo courtesy of Florida Game and Freshwater Fish Commission)

I believe a bear's vision is not as good as ours, but it is good enough to cost you a kill if you don't take measures to keep one from seeing you. If you freeze when a feeding bear looks your way, and you are not wearing some brightly-colored, highly-visible clothing, then the bear probably won't be alarmed. A strange sound or even a strange shape he can't identify may not send a bear streaking for cover, but let him get a whiff, ever so slight, of our human fragrance and he will vamoose, pronto! You must hunt into or across the wind if you hope to have any chance at all of bumping off a bear. The sense of smell is the bear's number one early warning defense. If you don't take his ability to smell you away, you'll never even see him, much less hang him on your den wall.

I personally believe for bear hunting it is best to let the wind blow your scent away rather than use some sort of coverup scent to mask your odor. I do use commercial scents when on a bait or for those occasions when geographic features make it impossible for me to stalk from downwind. Given a choice, I would much prefer to stay downwind.

If you want to hunt black bears one-on-one without the aid of dogs or bait, I suggest you plan a trip for an area where bear populations are dense and some sort of natural food source will concentrate them in small areas.

As tough as it is to locate a hunting area that has bear sign in sufficient quantities to make a concentrated bear hunt in that vicinity practicable, the work has just begun. It will require Herculean patience to sit on a stand just hoping a bear will pass close enough for a shot. Even in the best of bear country, it can be a long and uneventful wait.

Bears like thick cover and do not like to venture very far out into the open, even when working a bait, and they will rarely cross an opening in wooded habitat if they can detour around it. Therefore, it is a good idea to do your trail watching where a well-used trail comes out of thick cover. The bear will probably bed down in the thick stuff and you can ambush him as he comes out or returns after a foraging trip.

Another advantage to watching thick cover that has evidence of bear usage is the fact that, if a bear is spooked by another hunter (which happens frequently during managed hunts on public land where there are a relatively high number of hunters in a given area), he will probably go straight to the thick stuff. Opportunities of this type are not long in coming. When a spooked bear hits the trail, he doesn't waste any time

The hunter who attempts to stalk a bruin one on one in thick cover is often rewarded only by the sound of the animal exiting the other side of the thicket.

Bears often leave signs of digging around stumps where they have searched for food. (Photo courtesy of Arkansas Game and Fish Commission)

traveling from point A to point B. If you are smart or lucky enough to be strategically placed on his departure route, the chance you get will be a fleeting one at best. So stay alert!

As I have stated elsewhere, a black bear is probably the most difficult game to bag without the aid of dogs or bait. There are a few places like northern Canada, where they can be caught in the open spaces of the huge blueberry patches in that country. Or they can be spotted on a salmon stream or beach in Alaska. Occasionally one can be surprised on the open slopes of the Rockies. But, the eastern hunter who goes after a black bear in thick, heavily wooded, eastern bear habitat will have to depend a lot on luck, plus above-average scouting talents added to infinite patience. I don't mean the patience necessary to sit for three or four hours. I mean the patience that would allow you to watch an area that is loaded with bear sign for days rather than hours.

As close as I can figure it, I have spent about 130 days deer hunting in bear country during the last decade. During that time, while sitting at stand, I have had two bears within killing distance; unfortunately, neither was in season! Sometimes I was not in the best bear country, but I was always in areas that had enough bears to permit an open season, so I have to assume they were present in huntable numbers.

To sum up, there are several components that contribute to taking a black bear by hunting one on one. Scout several prospective bear hunting areas thoroughly and select the one with the *freshest* bear sign. Select a stand site, preferably a tree stand if legal, to watch as much of the area being used by the bear as possible. Come early and stay late. Mask your odor with some type of strong scent. And don't waste any of your good luck in poker games—you will need every bit you can collect.

13

Dealing With Wounded Bears

If you hunt bears there is always a possibility that you will someday wound a bear and have to follow him up for a finish. A wounded grizzly or brown bear is second only to a wounded leopard as the most dangerous animal on this planet. The cat's lightning speed and camouflage coat (which makes them hard to spot as they lie in wait to pounce on their tormentor) gives them the edge. A grizzly or brown is just a shade slower than a leopard and does present a somewhat larger and obvious target.

Any scope-sighted rifle you carry into bear country should be mounted on one of the see-through type scope bases. This will allow using the rifle's open sights at close range if a wounded bear, or just an aggressive grizzly, tries to bite the buttons off your shirt. Even so, a big bear has the disconcerting habit of filling the entire field of view in a low-powered scope at close range.

Many of the brown bear guides who take clients along the dense

Always approach a wounded bear from behind and from an uphill direction.

brush of the Alaskan coast or the thick alders along the banks of salmon streams rarely have scopes on their rifles. Instead, they choose open sights and pack one of the big-bore magnums which spout little mushroom-shaped clouds when you cook them off. These include the .338 or .458 Winchester Magnum, or .375 H&H Magnum. They select these calibers, and choose open sights, because they occasionally have to back up a hunter who is facing a brown bear in the bush with a bullet in his hide and murder in his heart. In such situations, the experienced guide wants a rifle that aims quick and fires a bullet that will pierce a bear's carcass and destroy any bones it touches.

Anytime you take a shot at big game, there is something you should train yourself to do before you squeeze the trigger. Using some land mark such as a bush, rock or dead tree, mark the exact location where the animal is when you shoot. This can save a lot of time later in picking up the blood trail of any animal you don't drop right in his tracks. After you shoot, study the landmark again to imbed it into your memory.

To reduce your odds of having to follow up a wounded bear,

Brain

+ = best shot placements

The best shot to anchor a bruin should be placed in a shoulder, or even better, in both shoulders. The brain is a relatively small target, surrounded by a massive head.

practice extensively with the rifle you will be using at all ranges. And teach yourself to call your shots; that is, learn to develop your ability to be conscious of exactly where your crosshairs are when the rifle is fired. This ability will be invaluable in the field when you have hit a bear but don't find any immediate blood trail. By being able to call your shots, you will know you hit a bear even if you cannot find any immediate physical sign such as blood or hair.

Blood sign at the exact spot where your bear was hit is actually rather rare unless you are using a big-bore mag. Even with a large bore, early blood sign may be lacking due to the layer of fat that most bears carry between their hide and body (especially in the fall) and also because of the thick fur on a bear pelt. Both the layer of fat and the thick fur tend to retard the flow of blood.

While I am on the subject, very few people outside of the ranks of professional guides are skilled at following a difficult blood trail. I don't mean the type of trail where the bear is dropping large splashes of blood the size of a half dollar, but those trails that consist of blood drops that are about the size of pin heads.

It is unethical to learn to trail wounded animals on live game, because early in your education you will lose some of them. With some help from a hunting partner you can develop tracking skills that will rival the best game trackers.

Get yourself a plastic squeeze bottle, the type that dishwashing detergent comes in, and fill it with a mixture of red food coloring, cocoa, and water. Mix the ingredients until you have a liquid that is the color and consistency of blood. Now have your partner, preferably an experienced tracker, travel through the woods leaving a blood trail for you to follow. In the beginning he can leave small squirts for you

This photo gives you some idea just how massive a bear's head is. The brain occupies a small area between and just above the eyes. (Photo by R.J. Hayes)

to find and as your tracking skill increases, occasional drops can be substituted for the more visible splotches. Some blood sign should also be left on brush and tree trunks to simulate the passing of an animal that has blood around a wound but is not dropping any on the ground, which is very common in trailing wounded bears.

Another little trick in keeping up with a blood trail and not losing it completely, especially when sign is scarce, is to drop a piece of toilet tissue next to each bit of sign. Then if you should lose a sparse trail, you can look back over your shoulder to use the line of toilet paper, indicate the general direction of the animal before you lost the trail, and concentrate your search for blood sign in that general direction.

It is risky business to have to follow up a wounded bear all by your lonesome. Bears have the unnerving habit of pressing a charge while you are searching the ground for sign. If circumstances require that you track a bear solo, then you should spend as much time looking ahead of you and to each side, if not more as you do looking at the ground for blood sign. Don't become so absorbed in following sign that you forget to keep a weather eye out for the object of your search.

There should be one tracker and one bear spotter. The tracker follows the blood trail while the shooter carries his rifle at port arms with his finger on the safety, ready for a quick shot should the opportunity present itself.

Don't get into too much of a hurry and trail so fast that you cannot diligently search all the possible places along the track where a bear could hide.

Sometimes your eyes may not be the sense that reveals the presence of a bear. Use your ears also. Keep talking to a minimum and limit conversation to just those few statements that are necessary to the job at hand. Whisper.

John Long and Brian "Spinner" Spencer (of National Hockey League fame) were once tracking a wounded black bear in Ontario. The bear had been shot late in the day, and darkness found my two buddies still on the track. Both of them possessed flashlights, so they opted to follow the track in the dark. This is not generally recommended procedure, but John had about two dozen bears to his credit and Brian had been raised in British Columbia where he had hunted bears since his early teens. John was playing the role of tracker, and Spinner was responsible for making the first shot count. As I remember, he was packing a .340 Weatherby Magnum.

Shortly after dark, John got Spinner's undivided attention with a tense whisper, "That bear is close. I can smell him!" Well, sir, after that statement, old Spinner had more eyes than a tree full of owls! John was right; the bear was found dead eight steps away lying behind a thick bush on his stomach. He died lying and watching his back trail! If that bear had not run out of juices before John and Spinner got there, this little anecdote may have had a much more exciting ending. If the wind is right and blowing from the bear toward you, you can often smell a bear in thick cover before you can see him.

If you have a choice, never approach a bear from the downhill side. Sometimes you don't have a choice. A bear that is shot while on a steep slope will usually tumble downhill. If you are on the downhill side of a bear when it is shot, the consequences are obvious!

You can forget lung, heart, and head shots when you confront a wounded bear at close quarters. The head shot is deadly enough, but it is a small target in a massive area. The heart or lung shot will kill a

A downed bear with his eyes open is probably dead. If the bear's eyes are closed, he is only stunned or knocked out. If the eyes are open, watch for any signs of life. If they flicker, move, or blink, shoot again.

bear, but he may live just long enough to bat the marksman around the woods, hurting the man and the landscape. The only smart shot at a wounded bear, or any kind of bear for that matter, is one that is placed to break one or both front shoulders. A bear that can't get his nose out of the dirt isn't going to travel far or fast. Once you have broken him down, you can finish him off with lung, heart, or neck shots.

If a bear is down, but not dead, shoot him again. Oftentimes a bear will fall to the ground roaring and rolling when hit, even if it is not a fatal wound. This is all the more reason to position yourself on the uphill side of a bear, if conditions permit, before you shoot.

It is a good idea to practice some "instinct" shooting at close range targets with the rifle you plan to take on your bear hunt. An old auto tire rolled toward you down a steep bank is good practice. (Be careful that you have a safe backstop for your bullets.) Such practice is good bear hunter life insurance for the hunter. Remember: it is the location and the size of the bullet holes that anchor bears, not the noise or number of shots you can squeeze off.

14

Staying out of Trouble in Bear Country

If you hunt bears, you must go where the bears are. If you go where the bears are, sooner or later you will have some sort of confrontation with a bear. It may be nothing more serious that losing your lunch or some spare grub to a camp-raiding bandit, a little meat from some game animal you couldn't pack out in one piece and had to leave behind for a while, or just an impromptu meeting at a bend in the trail that scared you out of your wits.

Your encounter may even be humorous. It is rather difficult to keep your dignity when a bear has just sent you scurrying up a tree or forced you to swim a cold salmon stream.

Sometimes the roles can be reversed and the hunter becomes the hunted and rather than finding a bear, the sportsman gets found. There is a real possibility that an unexpected encounter with a bear could end in serious injury or worse. But if you are bear hunting and armed with a suitable caliber rifle then encounter a bear, I don't call that

A pair of cute squalling cubs in a tree can mean an irate mama bear is somewhere nearby. Get out of the area as soon as possible. Even if you are armed, you don't want to shoot a sow with cubs. (Photo courtesy of Florida Game and Freshwater Fish Commission)

getting into trouble. That is what you came to bear country for—to find a bear and shoot it or take its picture.

CAMPING IN BEAR COUNTRY

Most hunters do their hunting out of some sort of base camp. Camps, along with all their accompanying odors, offer temptations that most bears cannot resist.

You don't have to be out stomping around in the bush harassing bears to get into trouble. In fact, most folks who do get into trouble with bears are in camp minding their own business. Here's an example.

I was up on the Shungnak River in Alaska a few years ago to do a little grayling fishing. I was staying in a mining camp which was just a short stroll from the river. On my first trip to the river I was excited by both the excellent grayling fishing and also the enormous bear tracks that were generously dispersed in the game trail I traveled on and also the sand bar I fished from. Those tracks were as big as the hub caps off a Ford pickup truck. I am not ashamed to admit that the old kid spent about as much time watching the bush over my shoulder as I did watching the grayling rising to my fly. The story I heard when I got back to camp that night didn't help my case of nerves much either.

About two weeks before I arrived in camp, the cook had gone to the storage tent to get the makings for some meal he was preparing and surprised a big male grizzly who was also in the building and in the process of making a withdrawal. That pile of grub was probably the most food that grizzly had ever seen in one pile, and he wasn't about to share it with this puny little intruder in the white apron.

The bear roared, the cook screamed, and both bolted out the door, with the cook leading by several strides. The inhabitants had been seeing some big bear sign around the edge of camp, but they were not aware of any having been in camp before. But, like most smart people in the Alaskan bear country, they decided to place a few rifles at strategic places, just in case a bear did come into camp. One of these rifles was a bolt action .300 Winchester Magnum which was leaned against the wall in the cook house right next to the front door.

The cook who was being chased was married to another cook, who was in the kitchen when she heard her husband yell. As she dashed out the door, she grabbed up the .300 Winchester. Her husband was doing some pretty fancy broken field running but could not be expected to stay out of the clutches of that aroused bear for very long. The wife (she didn't weigh 110 pounds) shouldered that big .300 magnum and waited for some daylight between her husband and the bear. When she got it, she squeezed off a round and dropped that bear right in his tracks. Her husband told me later that the three of them had been so close together that the muzzle blast from that magnum almost knocked him out. When she shot, he thought the bear had taken a whack at him and connected!

They had to do a lot of explaining later to the game officials, who frown on bears being shot out of season. The cooks didn't get arrested, but it was touch-and-go for a while. (The wife was still getting a lot of static from the guys in camp about shooting a grizzly over "bait." The "bait" they were referring to was not the food in the supply building, but her husband!)

One of the most successful techniques in our part of the country for attracting problem bears to culvert traps consists of building a small fire at the trap site and then throwing some pork and ham scraps onto the fire. After the meat burns awhile, it is tossed up into the trap to attract the bear inside. Burning the meat saturates the air with the smell of cooking pork, which attracts bears from a long distance when it is carried on a moderate breeze.

In the Great Smoky Mountains National Park, where I spent some time backpacking into the field with some biologists during bear research, they use ham scraps that are seared with a propane torch to attract bears to traps. These biologists are experts on bears and bear behavior and know better than anyone else what will attract them. I think it is significant that these biologists use the smell of cooking meat. Is it any wonder that bears are always turning up in camp? More than one outfitter has had his camp wrecked when he and his client went off into the bush after bears and left a frying pan full of bacon grease next to the fire.

If you cook bacon and other meats in bear country, it will only be a matter of time before you are paid a visit. The risk of bears destroying an expensive base camp while hunters are out in the bush is so great in some areas that outfitters will have one of their helpers stay in the camp all day to guard it.

This past summer I had several bear baits out to test different baits, so I would frequently bring home large plastic jugs of bacon grease from the college where I teach. My five-year-old daughter was curious about why I was taking so much bacon grease to the woods. I explained to her that bears would eat bacon grease just like it was candy. She got the message, and since then she has called bacon grease "bear candy."

Whenever I backpack into bear country, I plan meals that do not require the cooking of items such as ham or bacon that will saturate the air with tantalizing aromas. I choose instead the dehydrated meals which require only the boiling of water.

It is a good idea to hang all items which smell good up in a tree out of the reach of bears and a good distance away from sleeping areas. I know of a backpacker who once went to sleep in the Sangre De Christo Mountains of New Mexico with some of that orange-flavored Chapstick on his lips. He was awaken in the night by a horrible odor. As he was just beginning to wake up, he described what felt like someone rubbing sandpaper across his lips. Now, he was jerked into consciousness when he realized a bear was licking the orange-flavored Chapstick off his lips. The teenager screamed at the top of his lungs and nearly scared that poor bear to death. In his fright, the bear fled with the backpacker's tent draped around him like a big baggy night gown!

This story had a funny ending; many do not. In unrelated incidences, two women were dragged from their sleeping bags and killed on August 13, 1967 in Montana's Glacier National park. In the same Park, on September 23, 1976, a grizzly tore down the tent Mary Patricia Mahoney was sleeping in, killed the woman, and dragged her off. In his excellent book *Killer Bears*, my friend Mike Crammond documents no less than thirty-five bear attacks which occurred in campsites, seven of which were fatal!

Because outdoorsmen probably get in trouble in camp just about as often as any place else, it is smart to adhere to a few guidelines in and around camp.

Keep food odors to a minimum. Pack out all garbage in sealed containers. Make sure empty food containers are clean and odor free. Store food in plastic odor-proof containers well away from your sleeping area. Sleep away from the area where you do your cooking. Don't sleep in clothes you wore when cooking. Use gasoline-burning stoves rather than campfires. Don't burn garbage in your campfire. Don't use perfumes, deodorants, flavored lip balm or other sweet smelling substances on your body. Don't clean fish or game near your campsite.

Never, absolutely *never*, feed a bear. A bear doesn't understand that you are out of cookies, and he will search you thoroughly just to make sure you are not holding out on him. That little cub who begs so cute has a mama around somewhere, and she may not approve of you getting close to her offspring.

In addition to camping, another outdoor activity which results in man-bear confrontations is hiking. You may be hiking into a camp or just walking out into the bush to answer the call of nature and be surprised by an equally surprised bruin. In the vast majority of cases the bear will turn and flee when surprised by man. It is those few cases when the bear responds by fighting that you have to worry about.

When moving about in bear country, try to travel downwind. This will allow any bears in your path to detect your scent and make an honorable retreat. I had a native Alaskan tell me once that the best way to avoid trouble with a grizzly that you had spotted, but was still unaware of your presence, was to just move to the upwind side and let him get a whiff of you. He can still smell you from a considerable distance away.

Many experienced outdoorsmen in bear country will go to great lengths to make themselves heard by bears. Many big game outfitters attach bells to the halters of pack animals when on the trail so bears will hear them coming and not mistake their hoofbeats for prey such as elk or deer. Hikers in national parks are urged by park personnel to attach a tin can with a few rocks in it to their belts so bears will hear them coming. Whistling and talking also helps prevent surprising a bear at close range.

Never set up camp in or near a game trail. More than one camper has had a bad experience as a result of pitching camp or bedding down on a major wildlife thoroughfare.

Another frequent occurrence is the confrontation between a hunter who has returned to the site of a big game kill to pack out the meat. Grizzlies are especially bad about finding a hunter's kill and claiming it for themselves. A grizzly who has confiscated a big game kill will usually react in one of several ways. He may depart when he detects your approach and you will never know he was there. He may growl and bluff in an attempt to drive you away from what he thinks is his pile of meat. The most dangerous bear is the one who detects your approach and waits in ambush. This is the bear that will do serious damage to the unwary hunter.

Some hunters return to a kill site to pack out meat without a rifle. They figure a rifle is just that much more weight they will have to carry. They rationalize that they will not be hunting but packing meat instead and won't be doing any shooting. This faulty reasoning has meant trouble for more than one hunter.

Approach a kill site from upwind and make lots of noise so you won't surprise a feeding bear. As you approach a big game kill, look for signs of a bear's presence. Has the carcass or offal been moved or disturbed since you were last there? Has the carcass or offal been covered up with leaves, limbs, or other debris? If you observe any of these signs, then you should have a rifle handy. Look long and hard before approaching the kill. Shout as loud as possible to scare the bear away. If you find the carcass has been partially eaten and covered up, this usually means a bear has fed on the kill and plans to return. It could also mean he has eaten and hasn't left but is watching you from behind the bush. If you are not alone, it is a good idea to have one of the party stand on guard with a rifle ready.

Karl and Eric Braendel were sheep hunting in the Wrangel Mountains of Alaska and were lucky enough to have some sheep haunches cooling in their meat tent. Now sheep haunches are just about the tastiest meat you will ever wrap your teeth around. Apparently grizzlies also enjoy sheep haunches because one came onto Karl and Eric's camp and hauled off both their meat and the tent!

Karl and Eric awoke about 2:00 a.m. to discover their meat and meat tent gone. As they got out of their sleeping tent the grizzly returned for another course. Fortunately they were armed, and a shot sent the grizzly packing. These two hunters were mighty lucky; the distance between the meat tent that was raided by the grizzly and the sleeping tent was a mere three feet! This incident is proof that just keeping meat in camp does not reduce the chance of it being eaten by bears. It does increase the chances of the hunters being eaten along with their game meat!

While I am on the subject, guide Gary Ginther has a very good rule in his bear camps: if a bear comes into camp, the clients don't do any shooting; Gary is responsible for getting the bear out of camp. This makes a lot of sense. The risk of bodily harm and death by an errant bullet is greater when you have several guys in the same campsite shooting at a bear whose sole purpose for being in camp is simply to swipe some grub.

On many trips to bear country I have taken a break from hunting to do a little fishing. In northern Ontario once, John Long, Brian Spencer, and I had taken a break from the rigors of bear hunting to do a little brook trout fishing. To get to the little stream we were planning to fish we had to work our way down into a thick, brush-covered ravine. When we reached the stream and began to assemble our rods, I noticed a small tackle box on the bank with its contents strewn all around. Nearby I saw a broken rod with the reel still attached. I told John it looked as if someone had lost his tackle. John grinned and told me that the tackle had not actually been lost—abandoned was a more accurate description of the incident.

He proceeded to tell me the story of how a fisherman on this same stream had been surprised by a sow and three cubs the previous summer. The sow charged the fisherman, and he departed with haste, scattering his tackle in the process.

I could hardly fish as I was watching the bush for bears. Seeing an overturned log where bears had been hunting grubs and insects every few hundred yards as we worked our way back to the truck at dusk only increased my apprehension. This little fishing jaunt was made without the usual .45-70 lever action I usually carry over my shoulder when fishing in bear country. I don't mind telling you that I felt rather naked without it.

I was less than two hundred miles north of Algonquin Provincial Park where three fishermen were killed and eaten by a bear in May of 1978. I knew about the bear attack in the park; what I didn't know until later was the park was that close, and we were in an area that was more remote than the park. I am going back to Ontario this fall for some bear hunting, grouse hunting, and brookie fishing, and I imagine we will fish that same little stream again. This time I will have my .45-70 along!

Anytime you are in bear country and it is legal to have a firearm in possession, I strongly urge you to have one. There are two very good reasons for this. First, I could fill ten freezer lockers with game I have seen while lighting my pipe, using the bathroom, laying on my stomach drinking from a spring, or just relaxing around camp. The bear that you see unexpectedly may be the only one you spot on what could be a very expensive hunting trip.

The second reason is to defend yourself in case of attack. The bear that is really serious about hurting you is not going to give you a lot of advance warning. The only warning you will get will probably be no more than a coughing-like grunt just before he tries to tear you

Bears are frequently found near streams searching for food such as crayfish and sala-manders. In Alaska or Canada they frequent salmon streams. (Photo courtesy of Ten-nessee Wildlife Resources Agency)

Park bears that have been panhandling or feeding at dumps are often more dangerous than wilderness bears because they have lost much of their natural fear of man. (Photo courtesy of Tennessee Wildlife Resources Agency)

apart. The only bear that ever really tried doing this to me didn't make a sound. He just stood up from a bush he was hiding in with his lips curled back, his ears laid down against his neck, and all the hair on his neck pointing straight up. Luckily I spotted him before he came out of the bush, and I was ready to shoot when he made his move. I hit him in the middle of his chest, hoping to break his back, with a .50-caliber Maxiball, and he still made it about ten steps past where I was standing when I fired.

If you are not actually hunting, or it is illegal to have a rifle with you in bear country, then a .44 magnum handgun is the next best choice. If you plan to pack a handgun, learn to shoot it well. It is mighty easy to miss a bear, even at ultra close range, when he has scared you so badly that all your sporting courage has turned to jello. The best place to shoot at a bear that is on all fours and charging you is right in the nose. It is a mistake to try and shoot a bear between the eyes because most of his forehead and what appears to be the top of his head is nothing but long thick fur. If you hit him in the nose, however, he is a dead bear because the bullet will then hit his brain or the spinal column just below the skull. If you are too low, you will probably still hit him in the neck. If you are real low, then you will get him in the chest. If you are too far right or left, you will probably break a shoulder and drop him long enough to whack him again.

Take your time (a relative word in this situation) and put your shot where it will do some good. It isn't the noise that stops an angry bear—it is the size of the hole and where you put it that counts.

I strongly urge you not to use a handgun on browns and grizzlies, except in the most dire emergencies where the potential for serious bodily harm or death are imminent. If a bear is doing a lot of loud growling and posturing, he probably hasn't made up his mind to charge. Shouting and shooting in the air may run him off.

Just taking a new pistol out of the box and putting it in your holster will not do the job. You must spend many hours practicing with a handgun to develop sufficient skills that will allow you to place your shots in a vital area. Even the most powerful handguns are marginal weapons when using them on the big bears, so precise shot placement is the only way you will ever be able to use one with satisfactory results.

Eternal vigilance is said to be the price of liberty. Eternal vigilance is also the price of staying out of trouble in bear country.

15

The Second Season

Unlike hunters who hunt antlered game, the bear hunter usually has two big game seasons—one in the spring and one in the fall.

It is often easier to book a spring hunt in those states and provinces where there is good bear hunting than in the fall, when a swarm of hunters are scheduling package hunts for bear and antlered game. The guide who offers spring bear hunts is more apt to be a bear hunting specialist who will probably offer you a better chance at a decent bear.

The black bear hunter can choose from the following states when planning a spring bear hunt: Alaska, Montana, Wyoming, Colorado, and Utah.The Canadian provinces which offer spring black bear seasons are Alberta, British Columbia, New Brunswick, Northwest Territories, Ontario, Quebec, and Yukon Territory.

The grizzly hunter who wants to go on a spring hunt has fewer places to choose from: Alberta, British Columbia, Yukon Territory, and Alaska. The brown bear hunter only has one choice: Alaska. All polar bear hunting is done in the spring in the Northwest Territories.

The success of a spring bear hunt is very dependent upon the weather and the exact time that spring turns to summer when the bears come out of their dens. If you guess wrong and go too early and spring is still in the clutches of winter, you may not have any bears to hunt. They will all be tucked snugly in their dens while we hunters are stomping around in the snow freezing our butts off. If you guess too far the other way and your spring hunt runs into warm weather, then most pelts will be rubbed, and useless as trophy rugs.

Last year my spring bear hunt to northern Ontario came within one day of being too early. We had a dozen baits out and the black bears were only hitting them sporadically every other day or so. It was mid May, and the snow had only been off the ground for about two weeks. I was getting frantic. Seven of us had not seen a bear by the last day of my hunt. I was more than a little discouraged as I was finishing up my last day. As I walked into my stand late on the last afternoon of my hunt, I surprised a bear, which I promptly flattened. He had the longest, glossiest, most luxuriant pelt of any bear I have yet taken. I have killed bigger blacks—he only weighed about 200 pounds—but he made a high quality rug. I have a spring hunt booked for Ontario in a few months, but this time I am going a week later in hopes that more bears will be active and the pelts will still be prime.

When I went on a spring hunt in Colorado, I asked my guide what portion of the season offered the best chance of bagging a bear. He suggested the first week in July. He was right. Everyone in our party had a bear within three days of hitting camp, but there were rub marks on the pelts! The warm weather had made these bears do some vigorous scratching and butt rubbing. Consequently, the pelts on our bears were not of the highest quality.

You will have to get your priorities straight when you go on a spring hunt. If you go too early, you may see few, if any, bears. On the other hand, you will see more bears at the end of the season, but the pelts will be rubbed and have bare spots. You can expect a late season bear pelt to shed even more hair when the skin is tanned.

There are few absolutes when it comes to bear hunting, and this is especially true of selecting the best time for a spring hunt. Tell your guide what your priorities are. Do you want a prime pelt at the risk of not scoring? Or do you want the best odds at getting a bear, even if the hide may be less than ideal?

No matter where you hunt in the north country in the spring, go prepared to be eaten alive—by bugs! Take two of everything in your bug defense arsenal—two headnets, two supplies of bug dope, and a handful of heavy rubber bands to put around the bottom of your trousers to keep the bloodthirsty varmints from climbing up your legs.

You have to use every method at your disposal to make yourself absolutely impregnable to bugs if you expect to shoot a springtime black bear over a bait. A bear will never come into shooting range if you are so busy swatting blackflies that you look like a traffic cop on Times Square during rush hour. You must be still and not be going through a nonstop drill consisting of wiping bugs out of your mouth, nose, or ears.

Most spring grizzly hunting consists of glassing open, grassy areas, scouting or watching streams containing spawning salmon, or watching the carcass of a winter-killed big game animal. Grizzly country is invariably rough country. Travel is usually limited to horse back or hoofing it. In either case you had better be conditioned for either type of travel. The success of your multi-thousand-dollar grizzly hunt will probably depend on how well you can get around in the country and how well you can shoot. You can tip the odds in your favor by starting a vigorous training program in both physical conditioning and shooting.

Spring hunts for brown bear are often made in a boat that is used to cruise the coast. Once a bear is spotted, the hunters go ashore for a stalk. This sounds like a real soft type of hunting, and I will admit that it beats stumbling around on the banks of a salmon stream, but you still have to contend with the wet weather and cold temperatures of an Alaskan spring.

Many brown bear guides have some favorite salmon streams where brown bears collect. This is a most exciting way to hunt the giant brown bear. The only way you can travel through the thick alders that grow along most salmon streams is to walk on game trails. (I don't have to tell you what type of big hairy beast made those trails, do I?)

I cannot overemphasize the importance of total, absolute vigilance when sneaking along a streamside game trail. A rifle slung over the shoulder could cost you more than a trophy—it could cost you your good health. The rushing water of a salmon stream effectively drowns out any sounds you might make, and if you get the wind right a bear won't be able to smell you, so the only way he can detect you is to see you. And since vision is the only way you can detect his presence, it boils down to a fifty-fifty chance of who sees who first. Those are mighty stimulating odds when your opponent stands two feet taller than you and is strong enough to slap the tires off a Mack truck.

Any encounter you have on a salmon stream will probably be a close one. Don't assume that if you come up on a bear that is across a stream the stream will provide any sort of defensive barrier for you. Any chance you have in the close quarters of a streamside game trail will be of a short duration. The bear will go in one of two directions: straight away from you or straight at you.

Polar bears are hunted mostly in the months of February, March, and April (it could hardly be called spring hunting). Ice conditions determine to a great extent the success of a polar bear hunt by dog sled on the arctic ice. This trip will require a wait of a year or two as hunting opportunities are limited and the waiting list is long.

A spring bear hunt can range from a budget black bear hunt in eastern Canada to a polar bear expedition costing twelve grand or more. However, no matter what brand of spring bear hunting you select, you can bet it will stir the blood and tone the body more than any other spring tonic available.

16

Field Care of Meat and Trophies

A bear can be the source of many trophies and mementos and some memorable meals. Negligence in the field and improper handling of hide and carcass can eliminate the possibilities of both trophies and meat.

A bear should be field dressed and the carcass cooled as soon as the bear is dead. This can be delayed for a short period of time for some on-the-spot-photos, which should certainly be on your list of mementos of your hunt. However, I once lost the meat of a 300-pound cinnamon bear in the Rockies because I waited overnight to get some pictures. It was late June, and I should have skinned and quartered that bear or even gotten him to a cooler to save the meat. I was so intent on getting some good pictures, I lost several hundred pounds of prime meat. So be careful!

Quick cooling is essential to palatable bear meat. A bear has a thicker build than most big game animals of the same weight. Therefore it is smart to skin the bear and quarter it to speed up the cooling out process. I once saw an old-time bear hunter in the Appalachian Mountains in western North Carolina who had gutted a bear and placed it face down on a big rock that stuck up out of a cold mountain stream. The day was rather warm, but that creek and the rock that was in it were icy cold. I am sure that big cold rock was literally sucking the heat out of that bear's abdominal cavity.

Obviously if you are going to hang a carcass or quarters to cool, it is best to put them in the shade. If it is warm enough for flies, it would be wise to cover the meat with a cheesecloth bag. In extremely warm weather, you may want to place a bag of ice inside the abdominal cavity to speed up the cooling process.

If the weather has been cold but it warms up during the day, you can reduce and maintain a lower meat temperature by uncovering the meat at night and covering it with a tarp during the day.

Never haul a bear or any other big game on the hood of a car.

Bears, like all big game animals, should never be hauled on the hood of a car where engine heat will quickly spoil the meat. This bear was hauled on the spare tire of a motor home.

This method of transportation may provide maximum visibility for your trophy, but nothing spoils meat faster than the heat of a car engine.

Many hunters could care less about a big pile of bear meat; their prime motivation for hunting bears is a bearskin rug. The first step in procuring a bearskin rug is to select an animal that has a prime pelt. Bear pelts are at their best in very early spring, right after they come out of the den, and again in late fall just before they go back into hibernation. If you are after a prime pelt, then plan your hunt accordingly.

In some states and provinces, bear season is set up to coincide with the other big game seasons in late summer or early fall. But just about any bear you bag in August is going to have a pelt that will look like you dragged it all the way home behind your car! In states and provinces that offer spring bear hunts in addition to fall hunts, the spring hunts may be the best choice. Try to plan your hunt just after the bears become active. This choice is fraught with risk since a late spring thaw could delay the emergence of the animals from their winter dens. If this happens because you guessed wrong and planned your hunt too early, you won't see any bears.

The chances of bagging a bear are probably best during late spring and early fall when the bears are most active. In either case you are playing percentages and can only make an educated guess.

Just finding a bear with a prime pelt does not assure you of a beautiful rug. Bear hunting is just like most other big game hunting: the real work begins after the animal is down. Many a good rug is lost between the firing of a shot and the delivery of the green hide to the taxidermist.

Dave Elliott (Nature's Way Taxidermy Studio, 2381 Lockport Road, Sanborn, N.Y. 14132, phone 716/731-4215) has done some bear work for me that turned out very nicely. I called on Dave for the following suggestions on how to care for a bear skin.

Many life-sized mounts and rugs are lost because of bad timing in setting up the hunt dates and also improper handling of the skin. The best time to get a good pelt is the last month before they go into the den in fall. A spring pelt may be long and thick, but it could have some badly rubbed places from laying in a den all winter.

It is best to skin a bear on the spot where it is killed, if at all feasible. A bear is very heavy, and dragging it long distances over rough terrain can do irreparable damage to the skin. If you attempt to drag a bear over any distance at all, you can expect to have hairs

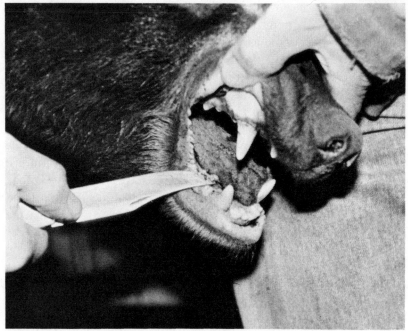

One of the secondary molars is being removed during skinning for submission to biologists to aid in bear research.

shaved off, loosened, and broken off. If you have a choice, skin the bear and carry the pelt to camp.

Skinning a bear is not a complicated procedure. I didn't say it wasn't hard work—just that it isn't complicated. The same method of skinning is used for both rugs and life sized mounts. Roll the bear over on its back and make three incisions on the underside of the animal:

A. Make one incision the length of the body from the anus to the middle of the throat.

B. Starting at the chest, make an incision toward the paw down the inside of the front leg. Repeat this procedure on the other foreleg.

C. Make an incision across the inside of the hind legs, reaching from paw to paw.

The incisions have a helical or spiral route and curve slightly from the inside of each leg until you reach the pads of the paws, through the pads to the toes.

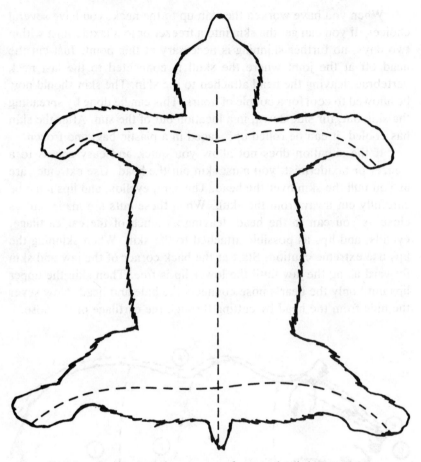

Incisions for skinning a bear (see text for more detailed instructions)

Skin the leg incisions until the leg bone can be severed from the hide last joint of the toe bones. If conditions do not permit enough time to skin each paw out down to the last joint of each toe, then the leg can be severed at the wrist bones and the paw skinned out in camp the next day. Skinning out the paws is a time consuming, painstaking procedure with no short cuts. The feet must be skinned out or the hide will be next to worthless.

A bear has a very miniscule caudal appendage (tail) and it is easy to overlook the small amount of meat and bone inside this tiny tail. Don't forget! After the legs and tail are skinned out, the rest of the pelt can be removed, working from the hind quarters toward the head.

When you have worked the skin up to the neck, you have several choices. If you can get the skin into a freezer or to a taxidermist within two days, no further skinning is necessary at this point. Just cut the head off at the joint where the skull is connected to the last neck vertebrae, leaving the head attached to the skin. The skin should now be allowed to cool for a couple of hours. This can be done by spreading the skin out, fur side down, in a location out of the sun. After the skin has cooled, it can be rolled up, placed in a plastic bag, and frozen.

If the situation does not allow you quick and easy access to a freezer or taxidermist, you must skin out the head. Use extreme care as you pull the skin over the head. The ears, eyelids, and lips must be carefully cut away from the skull. When these cuts are made, cut as close as you can to the head, leaving as much of the ear cartilage, eyelids, and lips as possible attached to the skin. When skinning the lips use extreme caution. Start at the back corner of the jaw and skin forward along the jaw until the lower lip is free. Then skin the upper lips until only the bear's nose connects the hide and head. Now sever the hide from the head by cutting through the cartilage of the nose.

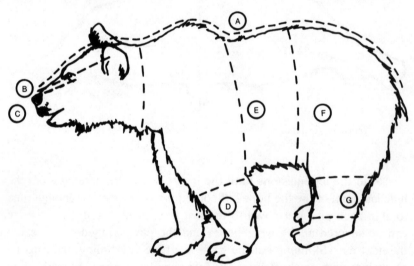

Take these measurements of a bear carcass after it is skinned to aid the taxidermist in preparing your trophy: A. Total length of bear, following upper body contour, from tip of nose to root of tail; B. Nose to ear orifice; C. Nose to eye socket; D. Circumference of front leg above and below knee; E. Circumference of body behind shoulder; F. Circumference at widest part of body; G. Circumference of rear leg above and below knee.

Now the fleshing process begins. Begin by scraping away any flesh, muscle, or fat that may still be attached to the eyelids, lips, and nose. Now the ears must be skinned out. This is accomplished by turning the ears inside out.

The cartilage of the inside of the ear is firmly attached to the skin. To facilitate skinning of the ear, use a blunt instrument, such as a screw driver, to separate the ear from this cartilage. A heavy butter knife also does a pretty good job of separating the ear from cartilage. Once you have loosened this cartilage from the ear it will turn inside out easily. Trim the muscle tissue away from the ear cartilage. The cartilage *must* remain on the ear so the taxidermist can make the ears look natural on your mount.

On the big bears the hide can be very thick in the region of the neck and forequarters. If the neck skin is very thick, the hide must be scored with a sharp knife. Score the skin by cutting partway through the skin. Do not cut all the way through the skin, just crosshatch the skin so the salt can penetrate the thick parts of the hide. Next you should scrape away all muscle, fat, and membrane that is still attached to the hide. This is hard, tedious work, but it must be done before the hide is salted. If any tissue or membrane is left on the hide, then salt will not be able to penetrate thoroughly and the hair in that section of hide will slip out. There is nothing a taxidermist can do once hair has begun to slip from a pelt!

The pelt is now ready for salting. There are a lot of ways to save money on a hunting trip. Being stingy with salt when salting a hide is not one of them. Salt is the cheapest thing you use on a trip, so use twice as much as you think you need, then use some more! Fifteen to twenty-five pounds of salt will be needed for each average black bear pelt. A big brown or grizzly could take twice as much. Don't use iodized salt.

To salt a hide, pour a big mound of salt in the middle of the pelt (on the flesh side) and use your hands to work the salt to the outer edges, making sure the skin is spread out smoothly with no wrinkles. Be certain to get a lot of salt into the paws and up into the toes. They will spoil quickly if not salted thoroughly.

Direct special attention to getting lots of salt into the head skin. Make sure the eyelids, ears, and nose are heavily salted. It is also a good idea to add extra salt to the hair side of the skin in the areas of the nose, ears, and mouth.

After the salt has been on the skin for from twenty-four to forty-eight hours, scrape all the salt and moisture from the skin and repeat the salting process. Now the hide can be folded, flesh side to flesh side, and left in a cool dry place. Place the hide so that it can drain. Don't compact it and don't put it in a plastic bag. If kept dry and cool it may stay stored like this for several weeks.

After you have skinned the bear, turn your attention to the carcass. There are some measurements that should be recorded for use by the taxidermist:

A. From the tip of the nose, along the top of the skull, down the center of the back to the root of the tail, following the curve of the back.

B. From the nose to the base of the skull.

C. Greatest circumference of the body.

D. Circumference of the body behind the front legs.

E. Height at the shoulders.

F. Circumference of the neck behind the ears.

G. Thickness of the body through the shoulders and hips.

H. Circumference of the lower and upper legs; all four legs.

I. If possible, save skull for other measurements made by the taxidermist. The taxidermist will return the skull.

The hides of bears should be shipped air mail or air freight after they have been salted and dried. The hide can be placed in a plastic bag after it is dried and then the bag is put inside a sturdy cardboard box and taped shut. Place in a container and notify the taxidermist that the shipment is on the way. Some areas require that the hunting license or game tag be attached to all packages containing any big game animal parts. Check local regulations to avoid confiscation of your skins! Try to plan your shipment so that the hides will arrive at their destination on a weekday to avoid being left in a warehouse over the weekend. This is especially critical if you are shipping frozen hides.

If your trophy is taken care of in the field, you will have something you will be proud to display for the rest of your life.

17

Trophy Bears

Defining trophy is as difficult as defining pretty. To a hunter who has never bagged a bear, any bear is a trophy. The first bear a hunter collects with a bow or a muzzle-loader may elevate a less than mediocre specimen up to trophy standards. The circumstances involved in killing a bear could be responsible for its trophy status.

The criteria for establishing world records are a little bit more specific when it comes to qualifying a bear as a record trophy. The Boone and Crockett Club maintains a record book for game animals killed in fair chase with firearms. The Pope and Young Club keeps records for game animals taken in fair chase with bow and arrow. Both organizations rate the trophy caliber of all species of bear (with the exception of polar bears, which are not being accepted since they are considered to be endangered) based upon the dimensions of the skull. The length of the cleaned skull is added to the width for the total score. The skull must not have been broken and repaired, and it must dry out for sixty days before being measured. For the score to be official, it must be measured by an official scorer of the Boone and Crockett or Pope and Young club.

The current criteria for minimum score to get into the Boone and Crockett Record Book is twenty-one inches for black bear, twenty-four inches for grizzly bear, twenty-eight inches for brown bear.

The seventh edition of *North American Big Game*, published in 1977 by the Boone and Crockett Club and the National Rifle Association, lists the world-record big game animals as of 1977. This volume is just about the best way I know of for determining which areas produce the most bear trophies. Even this system has its drawbacks since many factors can influence the ability of a specific geographical area to produce record-class bears. Such unpredictable and unmeasurable influences such as habitat modification, natural disasters, hunting pressure, logging, mining, or road building can literally change the quality of bear hunting overnight.

A bear, or any other game animal for that matter, needs several things in order to grow to trophy dimensions. First, he must have the inherent capability in his genetic pool to grow to trophy size. Second, he must have a habitat that is sufficiently abundant in commodities such as food, protective cover, denning sites, and some insulation from excessive human contact. And third, bears need time to reach bragging size.

The Boone and Crockett records indicate trophy black bears have been found in no less than eighteen states and seven Canadian provinces. In the U.S. the leading black bear trophy-producing states are Colorado with eighteen, Wisconsin with sixteen, Arizona with fifteen. After California with an even dozen, the other states have only a half-dozen or less. The biggest bear in the Boone and Crockett record book came from San Pete County, Utah and scored a whopping twenty-two and six-sixteenth inches. This bear was killed in 1970 by Rex Peterson and Richard Hardy.

A close scrutiny of the top ten black bears in the book reveals that four of them were taken in Arizona. Bear number two was taken on the San Carlos Indian Reservation in 1975; bear number three, in Apache County, 1968; number four, from Fort Apache Indian Reservation, 1971; and number seven, from Graham County, 1972. This data is of particular significance when you observe that all these bears came from a relatively small area in east central Arizona and, more importantly,

Judging a trophy class bear can be difficult since you don't have any antlers or horns to aid in the assessment. A trophy class bear will appear to have a broad head and very small ears in proportion to the rest of his body.

they have all been taken in fairly recent years. When you look at the next ten black bears in the book, you see that numbers eleven and thirteen came from the Fort Apache Indian Reservation and number sixteen came from nearby Gila County, again all in the same area in Arizona.

British Columbia dominates the grizzly records in much the same way Arizona dominates the black bear records. Of the top ten grizzlies in the book, six came from British Columbia, including numbers one, two, three, four, seven, and ten! That is not a bad track record. Five of the next ten record grizzlies are also from B.C.

Of the 237 grizzlies which qualify for Boone and Crockett minimum scores, 123 hail from B.C. Alaska is second with a very respectable total of eighty-five qualifiers. After first and second, there is a substantial gap before Alberta comes up with sixteen bears in third place. Montana ranks fourth with a total of five. The Yukon Territory and Wyoming are tied for sixth with four bears each in the book. (Wyoming is a moot point since there is no open season for griz in Wyoming. Montana's season is subject to an abrupt closing when the annual quota, usually about 25 bears, is reached.)

Biologists pretty much agree that there is no biological difference between grizzlies and brown bears. The differences are primarily in size. The coastal-dwelling brown bear reaches a much greater size, due primarily to the abundant supply of food such as spawned-out salmon. The interior-dwelling grizzly doesn't grow as large because of the restrictions of his harsher habitat.

The Boone and Crockett Club has established a line of separation between the coastal-dwelling brown bear and the grizzly for recording of trophies. Bears taken west and south of this line are recorded as brown bear. North and east of this line, bear trophies are classed as grizzlies. I quote from the seventh edition of *North American Big Game*: "The boundary line description is as follows: Starting at Pearse Canal and following the Canadian-Alaskan boundary northwesterly to Mt. St. Ellias on the 141° meridian; thence north along the Canadian-Alaskan boundary to Mt. Natazhat; thence west northwest along the divide of the Wrangell Range to Mt. Jarvis at the western end of the Wrangell Range; thence north along the divide of the Mentasta Range of the Mentasta Pass; thence in a general westerly direction along the divide of the Alaska Range to Houston Pass; thence westerly following the 62nd parallel of latitude to the Bering Sea." Now you know the difference in a grizzly and a brown bear—it is that little line I just described for you!

A nine-foot bear is rarely taken anymore. Most of the browns that measure nine feet come from Kodiak Island or the Alaska peninsula. You don't see many browns going into the book in recent years. I am afraid the good old days of an occasional nine footer are behind us.

Bowhunters have their counterpart to Boone and Crockett in the Pope and Young Club. The requirements for getting into the Pope and Young record book are similar to the Boone and Crockett rules inasmuch that the animal must be taken in fair chase, it must be scored by an official measurer, and it must dry a minimum of sixty days before being measured. The big difference is that the game must be taken with a bow.

Since it is much harder to take a bear with a sharp stick propelled by another stick and some string, the minimum requirements are lower for getting into the Pope and Young book. Minimum requirements are: twenty inches for brown bear, eighteen inches for grizzly bear, seventeen for polar bear, and seventeen for black bear. These measurements are taken just like the Boone and Crockett ones: width of the skull is added to maximum length of the skull without lower jaw.

You will frequently hear bear hunters refer to a bear that "squared eight feet" or "squared seven feet." You can be certain he is not referring to skull measurements. When a hunter refers to a bear "squaring" such and such, he means the length and width of the hide after the animal has been skinned.

To measure a hide, lay it out flat on the ground and measure from the nose to the tip of the tail. Then measure from one front paw to the other. Add these measurements together and divide by two. This method of measuring a bear allows for no small amount of larceny in tabulating a score. It isn't hard to stretch a green hide sufficiently to make a very average bear seem very above average.

To really get up into the trophy class, a black bear would have to square between six and seven feet, a grizzly of bragging proportions would square seven or eight feet, and a brown bear would have to get up around nine.

Judging the dimensions of a bear once he has been reduced to a pile of meat, bones, and hide is not too difficult. Judging the dimensions of a bear that is spotted on a nearby mountain or on the other side of a blueberry bush is a completely different matter. If you have done a little bear hunting, you cannot assume that a bear is a big bear just because he looks big. All bears look big until you have eyeballed a lot of them at different ranges and under various conditions. One old bear hunter once told me that the size of the bear is directly proportionate to how close he is to your person. A bear that looks like a hound dog is probably an adolescent. An adolescent human in his teens is long and lanky; so is an adolescent bear. That hound dog look is a dead give away.

If a bear's ears appear to be large, almost like Mickey Mouse's, then he is probably not a mature bear. As a bear matures, his head will get very broad and make his ears appear to be comparatively small. A male weighing approximately the same as a sow will have a much bigger head in comparison to the rest of his body.

If there is a lot of daylight between a bear's stomach and the ground, then he is probably not a very big bear. If a bear is so barrel-chested that his lower profile comes very close to the ground, then it is time to quit looking and start shooting.

It is often hard for neophyte bear hunters to look at a bear track and determine if the bear that made it was of generous proportions. Here is a little trick that will put you right up there with the pros when it comes to guessing the size of a bear by looking at his tracks: Add one inch to the width of the front paw track, convert this to feet, and that is approximately what the hide will square. If you find a set of tracks with a front paw print that is five inches wide, add an inch and convert to feet, which will give you a rough guess of a bear that will square six feet. If the track was made by a black bear, then he would be in the bragging size category. If it was made by Ol' Griz, you might be able to find a better one.

Careful observation of vegetation is also a valuable asset in evaluation of a bear's size. If you are watching a vast blueberry patch in northern Canada for a black bear, be aware of how high those bushes are. A small bear may look like a giant in new growth blueberries that have not reached their full size. The opposite can be true when a very respectable bear is standing in high vegetation. I realize that the bushes in a large field may vary considerably due to such factors as southern exposure, available water, and soil fertility. The smart hunter will scout as much as possible to be aware of these deviations from the norm.

18

Bear As Table Fare

The first time I ate bear, I was in someone else's house at one of those big game dinners that are so popular in the South. Even after I had eaten bear meat several times, I had no earthly idea what it tasted like because it had been excessively sauced, marinated, spiced, and overcooked.

Our first try at cooking bear meat was a noble experiment with the backstraps out of a bear I killed in Colorado several years ago. We merely placed the backstraps in a pan and broiled it in the oven, occasionally basting it with butter and garlic salt. We cooked the meat well done because I knew that bear meat sometimes carried the parasite trichinosis. I have since learned that freezing the meat at five degrees Fahrenheit for twenty days kills parasites, so now we don't cook our bear meat to death. Since that first experiment with what I expected to be a very strong, gamey tasting meat, bear has been a favorite at my family's dining table.

I now make an effort to get as much bear meat as possible home after a hunt. This can be difficult unless I collect a bear in the mountains around my home in Georgia or in North Carolina. When I fly on a bear hunt, I pack my clothes and gear in an ice chest and check the ice chest as luggage. Also inside that ice chest is a duffle bag. On the return trip, all my gear goes into the duffle bag, and the ice chest is filled with bear meat and dry ice.

I once had a fishing guide in Alaska warn me that the smoked salmon and halibut that I had packaged up for the trip home might not make it. Several of his clients had had fish and game disappear when it was packed in the easily recognizable cardboard cartons used by many outfitters. He solved the problem in a very ingenious manner. He acquired a supply of tape used by medical labs and imprinted with the message "MEDICAL SPECIMENS". He applied a few strips of this tape to all the cartons containing meat or fish and has had a 100 percent delivery record ever since!

I have already covered the importance of cooling bear (or any game) meat as quickly as possible so I won't go into another long dissertation here. I will reemphasize the importance of early cooling out of game meat.

I read in a history book how bear lard was prized as a shortening for pastry back in the pioneer days. I haven't tried bear lard in making pastry (I am not much of a pastry chef), but I did render some bear fat into lard to use as a lubricant for loading patched round balls in my muzzle-loading rifles. The lard was pure white and very hard when cooled. It had a pleasant odor, which surprised me, and it made a dandy authentic pioneer-type lubricant for my loads.

If you want to try your hand at rendering bear fat into lard for muzzleloader lube or for pioneer pastry making, it is very easy to do. Just get a large boiler or sauce pan and cut some bear fat into small chunks about one inch square and place it in the pan. Turn on a medium heat. As the fat heats up, a clear grease will run out. If the fat begins to smoke, turn the heat down. After the grease has been cooked out of the fat, pour it through a strainer and place into canning jars to cool. I plan to try some bear lard in pastry or biscuits the next time I bag a bruin.

Bear sausage is popular with European hunters who hunt black bears in Ontario. Many German hunters have their entire bear processed into sausage. It is not difficult to make. Mix ten pounds of coarsely ground bear meat, two pounds of beef suet (your local meat market will often give you extra suet they cannot use), and a half a pound of hog maws. Grind this up with one tablespoon of salt, two tablespoons of black pepper, and two tablespoons of sage. Mix thoroughly and put in the refrigerator overnight. Mix again the next day, divide into suitable portions, and freeze.

I strongly recommend that, if you hunt big game very much, you set yourself up for some serious sausage making and smoking. We have three portable smokers and are in the process of building a log smokehouse for smoking venison, bear, and wild hog. There is no limit to the variety of meats you can make from wild game, including sausage, smoked bacon, and even country-cured hams, with just a minimum of equipment and space.

One of the best sausage making and meat smoking catalogs I have run across comes from The Sausage Maker, 177 Military Road, Buffalo, New York 14207. And if you want to cure a few bear hams country-style, I suggest you write for the pamphlet "Curing Georgia Hams, Country Style" available from the Cooperative Extension Service, Georgia Department of Agriculture, State Capitol, Atlanta, Georgia 30334.

It would be very easy to insert page after page of pirated recipes and pass them off as unique and original dishes conjured up in our own kitchen. But I will simply give you the source of all our bear dish recipes. Just substitute bear meat for pork in your favorite pork recipe. We also like to cook bear roasts in the commercial baking bags.

19

The Future of Bear Hunting

Bear populations are probably in better shape now than they have been at any other time in this century, with the possible exception being the polar bear which is currently coming back from near-extinction. Black bear numbers are certainly at all-time highs for the lower forty-eight states. This does not mean that the future is promising for bears. The daily encroachment of civilization into bear country is a threat to their continued prosperity.

In some locales, the destruction of denning trees as a result of clear cutting timber harvests is a definite threat to black bears. A request is pending with the U.S. Forest Service to allow biologists to mark potential or known denning trees and not allow them to be cut. These trees are practically worthless commercially since they are always hollow.

Poachers are continually a threat, not only to black bears, but grizzlies also. Hundreds of bears are taken each year by poachers who

Bears need substantial chunks of suitable habitat if they are to thrive and be enjoyed by future generations. Denning trees, for example, must be preserved as they are vital to successful cub rearing in many of the eastern ranges. (Photo courtesy of Arkansas Game and Fish Department)

want to sell the fur, gall bladder, claws, and skulls. In some states the estimated poacher kill exceeds the total legal kill by law-abiding sport hunters.

Problem bears, panhandler bears, and spoiled bears are all names given to bruins in different parts of the country that have lost their fear of man and eat his bees, crops, garbage, and his picnic lunch. A rural family can see a whitetail deer cross the pasture and not get excited, but let a bear stroll through the south forty and they yell for the National Guard. I don't deny that a man has the right to protect his crops, livestock, and his family from wild beasts. But in many cases there are solutions to problem bears other than a rifle.

It is common practice in every state that has a bear population for the game and fish personnel to set traps to remove bears to unpopulated areas. This transplanting of problem bears serves two purposes: it removes the bears and puts them back into remote wilderness habitats where they can become a part of a breeding population.

A wildlife biologist in the Great Smoky Mountains National Park darts a black bear to take samples of blood, teeth, and tissue in an effort to learn more about bears and improve management techniques.

Up until ten to fifteen years ago, some states considered black bears to be vermin and offered bounties and no closed seasons. In Canada, the black bear has just been recognized in recent years as a valuable natural resource that will attract nonresident hunters and boost local income in remote areas which depend on hunters and fishermen.

Recent years have also been an intensification of bear management research and the implementation of intensive bear management programs. (I have had the opportunity to go into the field with biologists in Alaska and the Great Smoky Mountains National Park.) Many positive and negative aspects of bear management are now being studied. This interest and enthusiasm didn't really get cranked up in most states until the late 1960s and early 1970s. Major gains have been made in the last decade and a half, which is very encouraging for the future of bears.

Unfortunately, some warning signs are also on the horizon. Habitat destruction looms as the number one threat to bears being able to thrive. Included in this habitat requirement is relative freedom from human-bear encounters. The intensive backcountry use of Yellowstone and

Biologists take specimens and tattoo an identification number on a bear's lip. (Photo courtesy of Vermont Fish and Game Department)

Glacier National Parks will probably be the major contributing factor to the final reduction of grizzly bears in the lower forty-eight. Poachers will then push this great bear over the edge of oblivion.

The coastal habitat of Alaska will probably remain wild and un-inhabitable in large enough chunks for the brown bear to remain stable. I have nothing but praise for the Alaska Game and Fish personnel and the job they have done. The real problem in Alaska, as it is most other places, is the unwelcome, unwanted intrusion of politicians who don't know anything about bears.

But certain game laws have also helped bears. Several decades ago, the polar bear numbers were decimated by hunters flying over the ice in a small, two passenger aircraft fitted with skis rather than wheels for landing gear. When a polar bear was spotted, the plane would land nearby and the bear would be stalked on foot. This type of "unfair chase" led the state of Alaska and Canadian provinces to set specific regulations that prohibited a hunter from hunting on the same day that he was airborne in any aircraft. This regulation, and the banning of polar bear hunting for many years, has been responsible for the return of polar bears in huntable populations.

Even though the polar bear is currently on the threatened list of the Endangered Species Act, it may be removed from that list if the species continues to thrive as it has in the past few years.

The return of the ubiquitous black bear to areas where it was extinct early in this century speaks for the resiliency of this species. There are many states that now have a black bear season that didn't even have any bruins in the 1950s. The establishment of many wilder-ness tracts of thousands of acres has played a significant role in the return of the black bear in the eastern United States.

We cannot rely entirely upon the efforts of biologists or regulations to preserve the future of bear hunting. Every person who is interested in maintaining viable bear populations should become a member of the National Wildlife Federation and their state wildlife association. You must stay informed on the issues that concern bear populations and habitats. Write your state and national elected officials expressing your concerns. Encourage your associates to also write their legislators. Virginia even has its own statewide bear hunters association. (Nice going, guys!)

Not just wildlife biologists, but also law enforcement sections of game and fish departments, deserve and need our support. I once heard

Only habitat preservation and sound management techniques will insure a future for this bear cub and his kind. (Photo courtesy of Virginia Game and Fish Department)

an old-time game warden say, "If we take care of our deer, turkeys, and bear, everything else will go OK." I suspect there is a good deal of wisdom in that statement. Report any violators of game laws that you are aware of.

The future of bears and bear hunting depends to a large extent on how informed and involved outdoorsmen are. Do your share to keep the thrill of bear hunting in our future.

Index